Praise for

A Joyful Intuition

"Patrick Marsolek has written a useful hands-on book guiding the reader into practical self-awareness through a series of sensory exercises allowing one to experience directly what the text discusses. Doing what this book describes will change your perspective."
- Stephan A. Schwartz, Author of *Opening to the Infinite*

"*A Joyful Intuition* is a must have for the beginning student of intuition. Marsolek walks readers step by step through the varied and subtle aspects of intuitive perception, which I sometimes find difficult to communicate to new students. I love the way Marsolek teaches readers to open up and start the flow of intuitive insight. This hands on guide gives practice exercises and resources so readers can meet and continue to explore their own intuitive selves, a truly joyful journey."
- Pam Coronado, Sensing Murder, Investigation Discovery

"Patrick Marsolek has written an exciting and informative book that will expand the bandwidth of consciousness into the most important of the seven different intelligences – our intuition. There are a number of practical tools and exercises provided to help develop and strengthen one's inner sensing. I strongly recommend this book for anyone who is seeking more depth and meaning in their life."
- Lee Pulos, Ph.D., ABPP Clinical Psychologist, author of *Beyond Hypnosis* and *The Biology of Empowerment*

"Patrick Marsolek's extensive knowledge, integrity, thirst for truth and desire to help others uncover their own inner truth, shines through each and every page of this wonderfully insightful book."
—Nancy Marie, author of the
I Create What I Believe! Self-Awareness Art Program and *Passage of Change*

"Here is a book that is both scholarly and practical. To me, this is the perfect balance of knowledge and wisdom. I highly recommend this book to both beginners and professionals in the field of intuition."

- Jeffrey Mishlove, PhD
Dean of Transformational Psychology
University of Philosophical Research

"In *A Joyful Intuition*, Patrick Marsolek has created an intuitive experience more than a book. He guides us gently and thoroughly into a deeper way of sensing life, of applying our attention to what's at hand, then finding what's inside that. He never talks down to us but makes each intuitive task fresh, simple, and full of childlike wonder. If you read this book while being fully in the present moment, you'll be transported into a true communion-with-reality that reveals a tremendous amount of hidden information, guidance, and pleasure."

- Penney Peirce, author of
Frequency, *The Intuitive Way*, and *The Present Moment*

"*A Joyful Intuition* is an excellent guide for anyone who wants to cultivate intuitive abilities. In lucid language, the author offers valuable information, wisdom and a large number of practical exercises to help the readers tune into intuition and lead a joyful intuitive life. This book is a companion that you can consult continuously to evolve your intuitive resources."

- Prabhath P, Creator of Integral Gaia Yoga and
Editor of Your Spiritual Revolution E-magazine.

"You don't just read *A Joyful Intuition*, you interact with it. The exercises throughout the book develop one's instinctual inner wisdom. The exercises help someone like me, who gets caught up in everyday life, remember to reconnect with intuition -- joyously weaving it into the flow of life. The book is informative for the novice as well as the experienced intuitive. Marsolek reminds the reader to be still and listen to the messages the body is sending. Reading the book was like participating in a course or conference without having to attend one.

- Gail Hayssen, Intuitive, Remote Viewer, Reiki Master

A Joyful Intuition

How To Access Your Inner Knowing For
Insight, Healing And Happiness

by Patrick Marsolek

Inner Workings Resources LLC
Helena, Montana - USA

A Joyful Intuition Copyright © 2010 By Patrick Marsolek. All Rights reserved. No part of this book may be used or reproduced in any manner whatsoever, including Internet usage, (except for brief quotations in critical articles or reviews), without written permission of the author.
Inner Workings Resources LLC, PO Box 1264, Helena, MT 59624

Publisher's Cataloging-in-Publication
(Provided by Quality Books, Inc.)

Marsolek, Patrick.
   A joyful intuition : how to access your inner knowing for insight, healing and happiness / by Patrick Marsolek.
   p. cm.
   Includes bibliographical references and index.
   LCCN 2009913698
   ISBN-13: 978-0-9769041-1-3
   ISBN-10: 0-9769041-1-X

   1. Intuition. 2. Self-actualization (Psychology)
3. Self-help techniques.   I. Title.

BF315.5.M37 2010   153.4'4
                         QBI09-600235

This publication is intended to provide accurate and authoritative information on the subject matter covered. It is distributed with the understanding that neither the publisher nor the author is engaged in providing professional medical or psychological services. Any use of the information in this book is at the reader's discretion. The author and publisher specifically disclaim any and all liability arising directly or indirectly from the use or application of any information contained in this book. If professional medical or psychological advice or other expert assistance is required, the services of a competent professional should be sought.

ATTENTION CORPORATIONS, UNIVERSITIES, COLLEGES, AND PROFESSIONAL ORGANIZATIONS: Quantity discounts are available on bulk purchases of this book for educational, gift purposes, or as premiums for magazine subscriptions or renewals. Special books or book excerpts can also be created to fit specific needs.
For information, please contact: Inner Workings Resources, PO Box 1264, Helena, MT 59624 - info@patrickmarsolek.com

Acknowledgments

I am profoundly thankful for having been led into the company of the following people whose guidance, support, encouragement, and love have helped me in the envisioning, writing and refining of this book: Raymond Worring, Whit Hibbard, George McMullen, Bevy Jaegers, Lisa Marsolek, Bunny Albers, Sam Taylor, Marc Scow, Troy Holter, Julie Ryder, Dolores Dawse, Kari Mays, and all the fellow explorers who have taken my classes and shared with me their stories, tools, techniques and insights.

To them all and the great spirit, my deepest gratitude.

Thanks to Coleman Barks for permission to print his translations of the Poetry of Jalal Al-Din Rumi.

Also available from Patrick Marsolek

Transform Yourself: A Self-hypnosis Manual

Hypnosis and Relaxation CDs:

**Meadow to Beach
Healing Waters
Stream with Binaural Beat Frequencies
Stream with Binaural Beat Frequencies and Chime
Self-hypnosis for Pain Control
Remote Viewing Inductions
Trance Drumming
Relaxation Techniques
Sleep-Trance Exploration
Personal Validation Process
Quit Smoking Now**

Table of Contents

Acknowledgments	5
Foreword	11
Introduction	17
Chapter 1	23
Doorways	
Chapter 2	29
Beginning Sensing; Shifting Focus; Imagining Space; Body Focus; Describing	
Chapter 3	41
Spontaneous Shifting States; Fascination; Personal Validation; Experiences at the Edge	
Chapter 4	53
Imagining and Perceiving; Direct Perception	
Chapter 5	61
Softening the Conscious Mind; Spatial Body Focus; Baseline; Beliefs.; Sensory Awareness	
Chapter 6	73
Sense an Object; Drawing; Drawing an Object	
Chapter 7	81
Layers of Consciousness; Trance; Trance and Sensing; Visual Focus	

Chapter 8	95
Further Opening to the Unconscious; Breathing Focus; Intuitive Perception; Feedback	
Chapter 9	107
Body and Ideomotor Signals; Pendulum; Basic Questions; Sticky Fingers; Using Your Ideomotor	
Chapter 10	121
Envision an Object; Intention and Perception	
Chapter 11	131
Clear Intent ; Allowing; Intuition - Target; Target Feedback; More on Feedback; Intuitive Process	
Chapter 12	147
Unconscious Messaging; Reaching Out With Intuition	
Chapter 13	153
Description Releases; Personal Needs; Future Sensing; Redefining Noise	
Chapter 14	163
Fascination; Charged Emotions; Unknown Others and Language	
Chapter 15	173
Drawing Senses; Precognitive Newspaper; Peak Experiences; Living the Process	
Chapter 16	181
Beliefs and Fears; Integrating the Body; Envisioning in the Body	
Chapter 17	191
Suggestion; Personal Suggestions	
Chapter 18	201
Levity and Affirmation; Intuitive Target; Entangled Thinking; Spirit Connections	

Chapter 19   211
Body Focus as Exploration; Enjoying the Present Moment; Sound Perception

Chapter 20   219
State Markers; Psychometry; Playing with Objects; Money Energy; Asking Questions

Chapter 21   231
Expanding Visualization; Immersed Experience

Chapter 22   239
Intention and Body; Unconscious Intentions

Chapter 23   245
Breathing into the Body; Body Touch; Refining Senses

Chapter 24   253
Conscious Description; Timed Sensing; Dreambody Peripherals; Peripheral Practice; Deeper Body Focus

Chapter 25   267
Deeper Questions; The Flow of the Space

Chapter 26   271
Natural Consciousness; Falling in Love; Personal Intuition Questions; Expanding to Groups

Chapter 27   283
Living Intuition

Appendix A - Targets for Intuitive Practice   287
Appendix B - Websites   291
Appendix C - Glossary   293
Appendix D - Bibliography   295
Index   299

Foreword

We live in an amazing time, one that has been labeled both transitional and transformational. One certainty during this volatile period is that change will impact your work, relationships, family, social connections and many of your every day decisions. In our 21st century, the pace is fast. You may feel stressed, overloaded, even burnt out from juggling multiple responsibilities. If I could penetrate your mind to find out what you are thinking at this moment, I imagine I would find these three questions:

How do I want to live?
What are my priorities?
How can I get back in balance?

The word balance resonates. It means becoming 'whole-brain'. I am a 'whole-brain' advocate honoring both intuition and logic as necessary companions. During these changing times, you are limiting yourself if you question with only your logical mind. To reprioritize and understand how you want to live your life, you have to use your 'whole brain' and see the whole picture. What's the secret ingredient for getting this perspective? Accessing your intuitive mind. How fortunate you are to have this excellent book, Patrick Marsolek's <u>A Joyful Intuition</u>, as a resource to help you access your inner knowing for insight, healing and happiness.

Let's clear up one myth at the outset. Everyone has intuition. Intuition is not a talent reserved for special folk, but a gift all of us use every day whether we acknowledge it or not. You do not have to wait to be hit by a bolt of lightning to proclaim, "I am intuitive." With individual listening and awareness practice, you will know what your intuition—the deepest wisdom of your soul—is telling you. While I write these words now, a memory surfaces. I am walking on the beach on Paradise Island in the Bahamas. The blue-green water is ever so calm. Small waves gently break on the shore depositing beautiful shells at the water's edge. Some are small conch shells. There are pine cones, sand castles and even a snail shell. This image triggers another memory in my brain of a favorite Dr. Jonas Salk saying:

> *"I wonder what my intuition will toss up to me like gifts from the sea. I work with it and rely upon it. It's my partner."*

At this moment, my intuition continues to be my trusted partner assisting my logical mind. Throughout the pages of <u>A Joyful Intuition</u>, you will also discover how your intuitive awareness, which is bubbling up in your consciousness, can partner with your logical mind processes making you more wholely present in the world.

As a teacher and as the author of books about intuition, I applaud so many features of <u>A Joyful Intuition</u>. The book is an awareness primer guiding you, the reader, on a personal journey, so your intuition will surface gracefully. As I went through each of the exercises in this book, I felt as though Marsolek was my intuitive guide and teacher. He seemed to be standing there leading me gently through each step. The exercises in this manual, while illustrating practical techniques, also teach about the cycle of awareness which begins with intent, flows into perception, becomes learning and growth and ends in self-reflection. The revelation at the end of each process is fully explained.

The first step to begin to cultivate your intuitive abilities is to become aware. Learning to quiet the mind and court receptivity helps you open the door to inner awareness and your intuitive knowing. I truly value <u>A Joyful Intuition's</u> basic process using the body focus. It invites you to sense and describe what you are experiencing in your body, heart and mind. This sensing and description helps you release any unconscious thoughts, feelings, or perceptions that you are holding.

Marsolek also uses his Personal Validation Process to release struggles or resistances in your body and mind. Then you are able to more effectively respond to your unconscious intuitive messages. These particular exercises are brilliant. They will help you acknowledge your subtle unspoken messages that are very much present and could otherwise block intuitive retrieval.

Unlocking the wisdom residing in your unconscious is a key to become more aware of significant and meaningful messages you may have previously ignored. For example, is it an accident that you suddenly get a stomach ache when you shake someone's hand? I have always maintained that your body is an intuitive antenna. Is your transmitter or unconscious telling you that you can't stomach this person? Throughout this book you will learn how to get your sensing living body to unlock your one-of-a-kind unconscious wisdom. You will experience how the revealing dialogue between your unconscious and conscious awarenesses can be both empowering and liberating.

<u>A Joyful Intuition</u> explains how accessing your intuition will connect you to your creativity and spiritual awareness. Many decades ago, when I started giving intuitive development seminars to business groups, people flocked to creativity seminars. They thought creative development would help them produce and sell their products. Sadly, they didn't feel the same excitement about intuition seminars. Many did not see the close connection between the two processes. But, as I have always believed, intuition and creativity go hand in hand. Intuition is the input or energy for the creative act. Creativity becomes the many-faceted output. This

manual will show you how to tap into your unconscious information for both intuition and creativity. Watching your creative juices flow is one of the many gifts embedded in A Joyful Intuiton.

Over the past three decades I have maintained that intuition is always right. I still stand by that statement. Your intuition goes astray when the culprits of wishful thinking, fear or projection come marching in. These subjective ego-based emotions are judgmental, while intuition in contrast, is neutral. For intuitive input to be accurate and clear, thoughts or feelings coming from the ego need to be released. I appreciate how Marsolek's exercises can help you become aware of the fear culprit. You will learn how to release this negative emotion and tap into your unbiased intuitive flow.

The exercises in this book gently help you get your conscious mind out of the way in order to enter a receptive trance state. That is what I call making an enTRANCE the right way. The word trance has often been fused with fear and uncertainty for a budding intuitive. You might ask, "What will happen if I you lose control and let go?" But there is nothing to fear. You are simply entering the kingdom of your inner self to retrieve spectacular and evidential information. The reward for letting go are huge. Marsolek with his professional background in hypnotherapy identifies markers of the trance state to make your journey safe and comfortable.

Gayle Delaney, a pioneer in the field of dreams, taught her students to describe their dream symbols in a naive and detached way. She proposed asking, "If I were from another planet, what would this symbol mean?" I was reminded of Delaney's suggestion as I went through A Joyful Intuition's sensory awareness process. You will be asked to shift from what you "know" about an object, into what you are actually perceiving as if you were in fact from another planet, to get an accurate read from your intuitive mind. This suggestion will help you.

Another brilliant mind and believer in intuition, Dr Albert Einstein said;

> "The intuitive mind is a sacred gift and the rational mind is a faithful servant. We have created a society that honors the servant and has forgotten the gift."

Use <u>A Joyful Intuition</u> to develop and honor your intuitive gift. Savor your intuitive journey.

Marcia Emery, Ph.D.

Professor: Energy Medicine University, Holos University, University of Philosophical Research
Author: *PowerHunch!, The Intuitive Healer, Dr. Marcia Emery's Intuition Workbook.*

Introduction

Do you want to live a joyful, healthy life in which you have access to your own wisdom, creativity, and insight? Regardless of where you are right now in your life, there are inner resources just waiting for you. You can start accessing your intuitive self, a part of you that is insightful and restorative and can connect you to a deeper sense of meaningfulness in your life.

You may have heard of meditators or yoga masters who have reached an inner peace and enlightenment and are purported to experience a joyful living state of presence. To reach this state, they've dedicated their lives to meditation and physical, mental and emotional mastery. For most people that level of discipline and focus is not feasible or practical. That lifestyle probably wouldn't fit into your busy life.

Yet, do you have to throw away your desire for wonder, joy and spiritual fullness? No. You can live and work in the world and you can be connected to the spiritual and energetic qualities that give you meaning and wellness. It doesn't take a radical transformation of your current lifestyle, only a shift in how you are inside yourself as you engage in the world. You can reawaken a part of your being that is vitally alive, creative and joyfully connected to the universe.

Imagine a woman living her life, following the values that

have been instilled in her, working for success, raising children, searching for a relationship that works, wanting to find happiness in her work and her creative expression. She is doing everything that she is supposed to do to be happy and yet she feels unfulfilled and disconnected. As time passes, she feels less alive. She has to work harder to sustain happiness while doing everything that "has to" be done. If you could look at the "color" of her life it might look like a gray shadow over muted colors. She would be asking herself, "Who am I? What am I doing? Where is the creativity and meaning in my life?"

Then imagine she has an encounter. She's walking through a park and she sees a small girl playing with a stick. This child is waving the stick and imagining it's a magical wand. She sees the woman and pauses for a moment before her. Then the child points the stick at her, smiles and says, "You are now a beautiful princess." In that moment, the woman forgets herself and plays with the child. She smiles and says, "Thank you." Then she gives the little girl a playful curtsy, as she holds the edges of her imaginary princess gown. The child runs off to continue sharing her magic with the world.

In that moment the woman has been gifted. In her encounter with the child's magic wand and smiling eyes, she was transported, blessed with happiness and joyful memories. She remembers the way she used to play as a child, wrapped up in her imaginary world of immense creativity, adventure and learning. These memories tingle inside her with an aliveness and a sparkle. In that moment her color shifts to a bright purple and a yellow, a brilliant white/yellow light streaks out over her inner world, washing away the gray muted tones. This color/feeling radiates through her as she watches the child running through the grass with open trust, creativity, and aliveness. The woman feels a warmth, a softening in her body, a sense of safety and ease permeates her whole being. She remembers images, sensations, and the energy of her own creativity. She remembers her sensory aliveness as a child.

What happens next? Does the woman shake her head, break the spell, and return to her normal way of being? Does she pay attention and recognize the importance of this non-rational feeling rippling through her being? In that moment she has encountered a potential, an aliveness of possibility upwelling into her consciousness. She has a choice how she responds to it. The appearance of these kinds of gifts in our lives is one way intuition informs us and enlarges us. Have you been given such a gift? What did you do? Did you pay attention?

In my life, I have gone both ways. There are times when I have chosen to focus on what my rational mind and my sense of duty told me was important. There are also times when I've listened to that other, creative voice inside me. Both voices are important. Through practice and attention, I've learned to value that creative, intuitive impulse while still living my life of responsibility and commitment. I believe paying attention to the vital energy and aliveness of my being has led me into a life of more joy, more wonder and aliveness, and even a greater sense of health and well-being. As I write this book, I know that I am still learning and discovering the nature of my intuitive self. It continues to be a path of delightful discovery, growth and learning.

Similarly, you can say "Yes" to yourself. The exercises and explorations in this book will help you relearn how to be present with yourself in moments of meaningful connection and aliveness. You can reconnect to a guiding, wise part of your own being. You can remember how to harvest the richness of the colorful, enlivening influences of the world that are always soliciting your attention. Do you want to paint your world with a colorful richness and fullness of heart?

Perhaps more importantly, you can learn how to open to the fullness of your living presence as you are living your day-to-day life. The woman standing in the park in a moment of wonder could respond with joy and color, with warmth and richness. She could attend to her gift, and carry that awareness back into her life, gifting her own children and her world while maintaining her responsibilities.

Right now you are living in a body/mind that is intimately interconnected to the beauty and mystery of the living world. You have a 24/7 existence that is incredibly rich in aliveness, safety and meaningful engagement. Even now in this moment, you are being bathed in vibratory colors, sound frequencies and physical stimulation that I believe is implicitly loving, healing and creative. Can you imagine what it would be like to live in that awareness on a daily basis?

This joyful life is not outside your reach. It's not something to be gained and learned anew. It is an innate quality, an essential, elemental part of your being that is already alive within you. There are easy, practical ways of shifting into health and well-being within your heart, mind and body. You can envision and live what would be the best expression of yourself on your path into the future.

This book is an exploration into ways of being and sensing that can bring this aliveness, vitality and clarity into your life. Essentially, this is a practice of coming into your body/mind with consciousness. Intuition is one name for this consciousness. You may also call it insight, guidance, knowing, presence, connection, or even spiritual awareness. Intuition is an instinctive knowing, a sense of rightness within us. It operates the way a wound heals or the way our bodies restore themselves at night when we rest. Intuition draws us like the insistence of a gently flowing river, back into connection with our whole selves. Regardless what you name it, you can experience a direct, intimate connection to all the guidance, wisdom, and healing, that you were born with. You already have that ability. Like that woman in the park, you can remember how you are always connected to a larger, loving presence. You can open the door to a joyful, unfolding of meaning, and becoming.

When you shift out of the seeking and doing of your conscious self, you can come into a perception and engagement with an ever-present flow of information including; sensation, thoughts, feelings, internal and external awareness, sensing of yourself and others, of physical and non-physical energies. Within this present flow of being you can connect with and perhaps rediscover the most meaningful and rewarding aspects of your life. You may think you're reading this book to learn something new, to find the piece that has been missing, but something else may be happening. You may become aware of a different kind of instruction - the inward structuring of your own being, that is already occurring.

When you attend to what is happening in the present - perhaps it's a smell, a physical feeling, or an emotion - you come into an engagement with what is alive in you. With practice, you can learn to allow this flow of presence to inform you, to enlarge your awareness and to guide you into the next meaningful moment.

The exercises in this book will help you develop your connection to the unconscious and untapped resources of your being. They begin with a foundation of simple yet profound techniques for becoming present with yourself. These techniques will help you move out of the linear, logical realm of conscious awareness and into a more balanced connection with your whole body. This shift is inherently healing and restorative. As you awaken your sensory awareness, your mind will become clearer, calmer and more focused. Your body will relax and rest more easily. You will be able to listen and respond to the solicitations of your unconscious, relieving physical stress, and living a healthier life.

This intuitive exploration will progress into inner sensing. You will develop flexibility in awareness and attention. This attentional training will help you increase your mental health and resiliency. As you develop a larger sense of yourself, one that bridges different states of mind and ways of knowing, you will become better able to respond to the stresses and tensions of every day life. You will have more core confidence and trust which are essential for mental and emotional health.

Lastly we will explore the cultivation of specific intuitive practices which you can use to access tangible information that relates to your world. In terms of personal health, you can learn how to perceive what your body needs for well-being, whether or not a certain activity or intention serves your overall well-being, or even what you might need to do to heal an old emotional pattern or habit. You can learn how to use your intuition to guide your decisions at home or work and to improve your relationships with family, friends and coworkers.

Are there specific reasons you want to learn to be more intuitive? Hold that intention in your mind as you read. Through the course of this exploration you will discover tools that will help you reach your goal. You will also learn more about yourself in the process. You will learn how your mind works, how your body is connected to your mind and your unconscious. You will learn which senses and perceptions are more accessible to you, and even how to move towards what you're wanting with less effort, more trust and joy.

So as you go enter this exploration, take a moment and make yourself comfortable. Ask yourself,:

> *Is there anything you need now to help you become more present?*
> *Would you like to turn off the phone or get a cup of tea?*
> *Why not begin taking care of yourself right now?*

Then, with a full sense of being connected to this moment, read on and open yourself to the next unfolding experience.

Chapter 1

Doorways

Opening the pages of this book begins your exploration. As you follow your intention to learn, expand, and grow you have already opened a door inside yourself. This doorway is a transitional place where you are naturally more engaged in the present. When you go through a physical door, you perceive changes in several different senses. What you see, hear, smell and feel may all be recognizably different. As you encounter these changing sensations you are more in the present, at least for a few moments. So it is also as you pass through the threshold of this book.

There are many kinds of doors besides the physical ones separating rooms. People you meet, new ideas, an opening in a landscape you pass through, a change in the weather, shifting states of consciousness, memories, even physical changes in the body are all new doors. You may not even realize you are going through a door until you sense something has shifted.

When you do recognize you are about to go through a door, pause for a moment and use that opportunity to heighten your awareness. Before entering, take a moment and notice what is happening inside you—in your mind, body, heart, and spirit. Do you feel a sensation in your body? Are you hearing sounds? What is the emotion you're feeling? Then, being more in touch with what you are perceiving, you can go through the door and be more conscious of the changes you experience. The changes you first recognize may be external perceptions, such as colors, smells, shifts in temperature or sounds. Having paused before entering, you will be more able to notice these changes. Yet, as you become more attentive you will begin to notice more subtle changes. You may sense a different ambiance in the new space, your thinking may take on a different quality, or you may even sense an internal shift in your own energy.

> *Are you already perceiving changes as a result of entering this doorway of this book?*
> *How would you describe these changes?*

Each time you see italicized words like this, take the time to attend to what these words are asking you. This book is intended to be used as a work book. As you put yourself into each exercise you will gain more insight and understanding.

As you read, have a pen with you and something to write on. Find a notebook or a journal that you can dedicate to your explorations with this book. The meaning you experience reading this book flows out of your participation with it. Each idea you are drawn into resonates inside you in a meaningful way. As you participate more, what you experience will become more meaningful.

You can consciously step through each door you encounter and become aware of the aliveness of the immediate, sensory world. You can with equal consciousness close this book, put it down and continue learning in different ways and in a different context. You always have the ability to choose what suits you. You have an infinite number of moments to listen to other ways of knowing.

> *What is this moment telling you?*

Enjoy an Image...

Figure 1

Observe this image. Even an image in a book may be a catalyst for another meaningful moment in your life. Physically, you have already responded to this image. The patterns of black and white and the shapes have massaged the cells in your eyes, triggering waves of information and electricity in your brain and in your body. In your mind, these energies and images may have triggered memories and emotions.

> *Take a moment and describe your response to this image.*
> *What senses are stimulated? Memories? Feelings?*
> *What thoughts come to mind?*
> *Are there other changes that you experience as you view this image?*
> *Be aware of what is alive in you now and describe it.*

By paying attention now, you are more conscious in this moment of the changes this picture evokes in you. You may not sense any particular significance to this image, but you do still have a response. Thus, this image is another doorway. As you pay attention to your response to that image, you send a message to a deeper part of yourself. You tell that part you are interested in other kinds of information. When you attend to your present experience, there is an inner portal that opens, an entrance into experiencing yourself more fully.

With each page you turn and each idea you encounter, you can become more open to the flowing present. You perceive an image, a smell, or a thought flows into you and your mind and body change. Perhaps the shape you saw on the previous page triggered an inner sensation or a memory of a similar scene you experienced. With that stimulus, a part of your awareness turned inward and opened. You can allow that subtle opening to inform you.

> *Of course, if you discount such simple things, if you're so unconscious of them that they're experienced merely as reflex and don't even cause a blip on your inner screen, then you won't be seeing shimmering, barely glowing orbs of light while you're making love either. But what are you going to believe, your own senses or how you've been taught the world works?*
>
> *- Michael Ventura 32* [*]

You become more receptive to intuition by paying attention to what is happening now. You cross over a threshold from what you know or believe in your mind, to what is occurring in this present moment. You may notice a color, a shape, or a sensation in your body. These are all triggered by the image. When you attend to these perceptions, you shift your awareness into direct sensing. Direct sensing is intuitive.

In the first few moments you viewed the photograph, typically for only a fraction of a second, you were in direct perception. Your awareness was observant and receptive, noticing contrasts, shapes and textures. As you recognized these things, your mind likely came up with a label for it. With that labeling, you probably shifted back out of direct perception into thought and memory. This rec-

---

[*]   Reference numbers refer to sources listed in bibiliography.

ognition and labeling happens very fast. You've been trained to do it; we all have. You've been rewarded for being able to understand things quickly and efficiently. The flow of direct perceptions is stopped when you label and define what you are experiencing and shift to thinking about it.

Staying receptive to the present is essential for opening the doors of intuition and for shifting into a healthy balance of mind and body. It is easier to be present when you are experiencing changing stimuli, such as turning a page, opening a door or perceiving something new. Experiencing new stimulus forces your awareness into the present for a few moments. With attention and practice, you can stay in the present longer without needing continuous stimulation. You can learn to stay present within the ever flowing change of your own consciousness.

> *Now you can let your sensing go a little deeper, with another visit to the image on page 25. Read this guide first:*
>
> *This time as you view the image, give yourself time to be present.*
> *Pay attention to the whole range of your experience.*
> *Take more time and notice the contrasts.*
> *Let your other senses engage with what is pictured in the image.*
> *What smells would be there?*
> *The temperature?*
> *The textures?*
> *What is the mood of the place?*
>
> *Imagine you could perceive what is pictured in this image without thinking. What would that be like?*
> *If you could put your body in that place, how would it respond?*
> *How would your heart respond?*
> *Your spirit?*
> *Which senses are the most activated by the image?*

Do it now.

Then write down your responses to your second viewing.

Whatever responses you have to that image are OK. There is no correct or incorrect way of perceiving. As you sit with an image and your responses to it, you may experience a movement. The movement could contain thoughts, activation in your body, a feeling of hunger, a need to move or stretch, or an image of a person you know entering your mind. Whatever response occurs within you, allow it and notice it.

What would it be like to allow yourself to stay with your responses to the image, even to linger with them for a little while? There may be something else that's guiding you through this doorway. You can attend to those solicitations.

Take a moment and reflect on the difference between perceiving that image the first time and when you relaxed into it.

Chapter 2

Beginning Sensing

I'd like you to begin extending and refining your awareness. I want you to learn how to shift into a more receptive frame of mind. To do this, you will shift to sense perception. First, become aware of how you are sitting. Then take a moment and address each of these questions internally:

> *Are you comfortable?*
> *Would it be OK for you to be even more comfortable while you read?*
>
> *Respond if you need to.*
> *You can make yourself more comfortable.*

If you sense a need to shift or change your physical position at the beginning, pay attention to it. What can you do about it? I'm not talking here only about relieving physical discomfort, although you can do that. Finding comfort is also about moving towards something. You can move towards greater well-being, even joy. You can move toward a new experience. Comfort may be active and passive simultaneously. You can do whatever you need to do for yourself, now, regardless of what it is. Change your position if you want to. When you respond to the idea of comfort, it may even cross your mind what it is you would like to be comfortably moving toward.

From the position your body is in now, I'd like you to become aware of the sense of hearing. Then you will describe those sounds. Normally when we pay attention to something, we're trying to put it into a mental box, staying with the labeling part of our minds. For example, if I were to describe what I'm hearing, I might write:

> *I hear my computer running, the clicking sound of typing on my keyboard and, occasionally, I hear a bird chirping outside.*

Sentences like these are how we normally describe something using the labels we have. For this exercise, I want to you go further into your senses. Stay with your senses. Take your time and describe it as if you don't know what it really is you're hearing.

Here's how I would describe what I'm hearing as I stay with what I am actually perceiving:

> *I hear a humming. It's a soft whirring sound that has a slower, regular beat. Now it seems to be more of a pulsation. There are also different notes in the humming that are hard to differentiate, some higher, some lower. There's also a rhythmical tapping and clicking sound, with lower tones and higher ones. It's irregular, with pauses, then flurries. Farther away, there are chirping sounds. These, too, rise and fall. They sound thicker one moment, and less dense the next.*

As I bring my attention to the sounds around me, it takes me a little time to allow my consciousness to shift from thinking to hearing. At first I know what I'm hearing, but then I gradually relax into the experience of hearing. The sounds become richer and more meaningful. As I stay with my awareness, the quality changes. I am able to enjoy this deeper richness without needing to define it. Some of my awareness shifts back as I compose these words on paper, but my perception of richness also remains.

Give yourself permission to enter your sensing slowly. Start to listen to the sounds around you. Be patient with yourself. You may not have words to describe what you're hearing. It may take a few moments. Take a deep breath. Relax. Enjoy the process. Allow your awareness to settle and deepen into what you hear. As you pay attention you'll notice more. Sounds will become richer.

Listen.
Become aware of the sounds you hear and pause in your reading.
Notice the qualities, textures and intensities of those sounds.

Then, when you're ready, describe those sounds to yourself.
Stay with the sensory descriptions.
Write down your perceptions.

Do it now.

How does it feel when you allow yourself to drop into the sense of hearing?

Whatever qualities you gained in your awareness, you can keep those with you as you return to reading. Your enjoyment of this moment gives you a powerful connection to your unconscious. The way you perceive with your physical senses is directly related to intuitive perception. Attending to sounds or any other senses you are experiencing with full consciousness becomes an experience of direct perception. It is intuitive.

You have many ways of perceiving, some internal and some external. All of them are ways of immersing yourself in intuitive knowing. Tremendous meaning can be triggered by a simple sense. Even a familiar sound can be the doorway to an experience that is deeply profound.

Shifting Focus

Every time you shift your awareness into direct perception, you are also altering your brain frequencies and your physiology in a healthy way. In your normal, analytical frame of mind, you are generating Beta frequencies. They are typically the most active and fastest frequencies occurring in our brains. Slower, Alpha frequencies are generated when we shift into a more receptive state of awareness. The slowest brainwaves are the meditative frequencies of Theta and Delta which are associated with deep relaxation or sleep.

When you come into your senses, you activate more Alpha and Theta frequencies in your brain. If you're experiencing stress, you will feel some release or relaxation when you make this shift.

In the book, <u>The Open Focus Brain</u> [16], Jim Robbins and Dr. Les Fehmi present an in-depth look at how the way we attend to the world affects our health. Dr. Fehmi, a psychologist and brainwave researcher at Princeton, has focused his research on synchronous alpha frequencies in the brain. These brainwave frequencies and sensations of health and well-being occur when we allow ourselves to engage fully into a sensory experience, one that is not directed by the conscious mind and will.

Fehmi found that there were two questions on a hypnotic susceptibility questionnaire that consistently produced synchronous alpha brainwaves in his subjects. Both questions had to do with imagining space. Every time a test subject was asked to imagine space, his brain produced more alpha. Fehmi theorizes that imagining space provides a simple way to force the brain to stop grasping in a habitual narrow focus and move into a more receptive balanced focus that he calls "open focus." I believe that any time we can drop into the sensory experience of the moment, as with the sound exercise above, we generate more alpha frequencies in the brain and can experience some of the same healing effects.

Imagining Space

You can get a sense of how this works now.

As you read, imagine you can become aware of the space in and around each of the letters on this page.
Slow down and do this while you're reading now.

Then bring into your awareness the spaces between the words.
As you continue reading you can also be aware of the space around the sentences and paragraphs.
As you're aware of the space, continue to be aware of the words and their meanings.

Can you also be aware of the space between your eyes and the paper?
How do you sense that space?

Can you expand this to include an awareness of the space around your body?

Keep the awareness of space with you while you continue reading.
Become aware again of the sounds you are hearing, while you are aware of the spaces and the words.

Is it possible to attend to all those senses equally, while you are reading these words and sensing the space?

Experiment with being in that flow of sensation and letting it inform you.
Imagine there is also space in your awareness, in between thoughts, senses, words, feelings, even as you are reading.

Notice how this way of attending makes you feel.

Describe those sensations.

As you do this exercise you may notice how the intensity of the words and their meanings alters. That awareness may now be combined with your sense of your body or other internal perceptions. These words are perceived in a greater context of spaciousness. They may not be as important, or their importance may shift. You may also have a different awareness of the sounds that you focused on earlier.

Let your awareness continue to flow softly as you attend to the words in front of you now.

When you allow yourself to become immersed into your senses (perhaps even into the feelings on your skin while you're reading), then you make the shift to a different way of attending and to different brainwave frequencies in your brain. Your attention begins to spread out. A healthier mind and body and intuitive sensing becomes more accessible. This kind of attentional flexibility is essential for your health.

Fehmi's open focus, hypnotic trances, and other consciousness states have been shown to bring about the remission of many stress related symptoms—chronic pain, insomnia, and even eye and skin disorders. People who have been primarily locked in to an analytical, cognitive way of focusing may experience the most profound results as they shift into a more immersed, sensory experience. You may not even know what stress you're carrying until the load is lifted.

Once we shift in a safe, comfortable way, our whole world can change. I often see profound responses with my hypnosis clients when they first shift. The process of going into trance allows them to let go of habitual holding. Muscles they never even knew existed may start twitching. This can be disconcerting and startling to the ego and might even be perceived as if the body has been taken over by another force. As the muscles release, spontaneous memories or emotions associated with the tension also become conscious. Through this release they reconnect with huge unconscious parts of themselves.

> # Attentional flexibility is essential for your health.

Releasing awareness from the confines of narrow objective focus frees up the natural flexibility of your attention. Sensory awareness anchored in the present becomes a meaningful unfolding of thoughts, sensations, and emotions. They are all part of the intuitive flow bringing your deeper self into consciousness.

Body Focus

I'd like to introduce you to a simple, yet profound practice to bring you back into direct perception and into a more fluid flow of brainwave frequencies.

> Read through this entire exercise before you begin.
> *Begin by becoming aware of what you are perceiving with each of your physical senses. The intent here isn't to analyze or label what you are sensing. Rather, it's to allow yourself to move into an actual sense of it, just as we did with the sense of sound. Be patient with yourself. Stay with each sense until your awareness embraces it. Every sense will become richer and more interesting as you let yourself embrace it. Your attention activates it.*
> *After allowing yourself to become immersed in the actual sensing, let your experience guide you back towards words.*
> *Describe what you are perceiving.*
> *Do it as best you can with words on paper.*
> *Describe rather than label.*
> *Take as long as you need to accurately communicate what you are sensing. If a word doesn't come, then wait; be patient. Take another breath. Go into the sense again until some way to describe it emerges. Go through each of your senses—smell, touch taste, sight and hearing—in whatever order appeals to you. Stay with each one until you connect with it in some way, then describe what you sense.*
>
> *Take your time. Enjoy yourself.*
> *Spend some time with each of your senses and then describe your experience.*
> *Then, after describing your sensing, notice what's going on inside you. Have there been any internal changes? Are you experiencing an emotion, a mood, or other feelings? Be aware of these responses. Then describe them as best you can; don't censor yourself or label your response.*
> *How would you describe your state of mind?*
> *How would you describe the emotion your feeling?*

Are you experiencing any other internal changes?
Describe all these perceptions.
Do it now.

As with the sense of sound, every channel of awareness we have can be full, rich and absorbing. The sensory present can be an amazing place when you allow it. As part of this process I encourage you to allow whatever it is you experience. Just describe it and stay with it. There is no right way or wrong way to do this exercise.

Sensing and describing what you are experiencing in body, heart and mind is the basic process of the body focus. Attention to your actual experience shifts you into direct sensing. Then you communicate what you experience. Here's a short example of the body focus as I'm writing. I pause, go into each sense, then write when I feel ready...

> *I hear a rhythmic sound, several levels, a buzzing rattle, higher pitched, also a lower hum. The hum I also feel in my body, more so in my feet, coming through the floor.*
> *Visual... white sheets, golden brown, lots of objects close, bright colors.*
> *Smell... slightly smoky, humid, body smells, warm, familiar, an earthy smell also.*
> *Taste... slightly chemical, neutral mouth taste, a sharpness.*
> *Touch... a sense of warmth in my body, stomach working, tension in shoulders, like a buzzing. In my hands, a smooth texture, that's hard and flat.*

Now my emotion is calm and my mind is more focused. My mood is neutral and lighter now. Hearing and touch are easier for me to describe. If I take a moment and go deeper into my visual perception, more arises...

> *Color... rich tones, yellows to browns, golden, several layers, sense of depth to these tones, a richness, it's spreading out with a calming effect. It has a natural feel and takes me outdoors.*

What you describe when you do the body focus is only for you and for now. It connects your conscious mind to your unconscious mind through the flow of experience. You can allow each sense to lead you into words that feel right. The following figure illustrates the different channels of awareness you may embody at any moment. When you do the body focus, you can go into any or each of these channels. They are separated into internal and external channels but they are all in your consciousness. The word proprioception at the top of the figure refers to any internal body sensations including pain, movement, and balance. At first, it may be easier to start your body focus by focusing on the external senses.

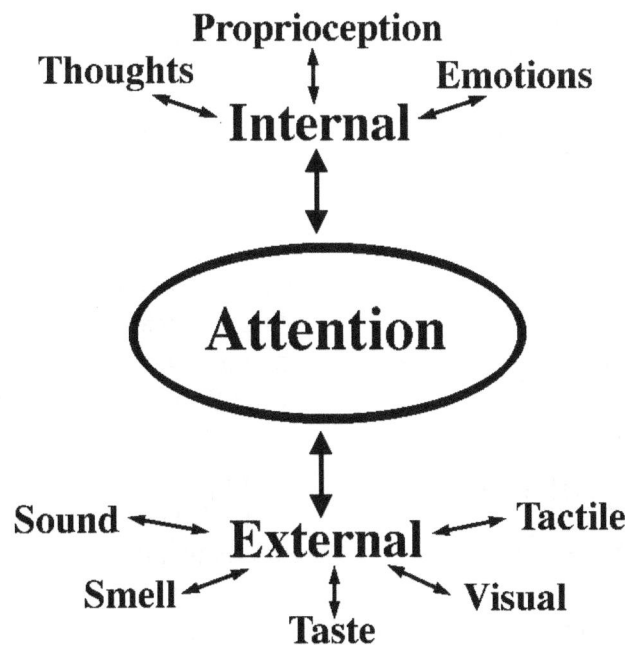

Figure 2- Body Focus

Obviously, by calling this process a body focus, I'm expanding the definition of body. I'm calling the entire form you inhabit including your thoughts, feelings and non-physical energies your body. All of these channels of awareness make up what you experience in any given moment. Through this flowing body you experience your world.

Each time you do the body focus, you can allow yourself to "go into" anything you perceive. You can stay with a sensation long enough for your awareness to merge with it. Then you can describe it. Your description doesn't have to be perfect. All you have to do is describe what you experience as you are aware of it.

Because there is no right or wrong to the flow of your awareness, I would like you to use a pen as you do the exercises in this book. Communicating your experience as it is is important. You don't need to erase anything. Erasing something means you didn't get it right. If something becomes clearer after you write, then write or describe more to clarify it. The second word may feel more accurate but the both represent your process of unfolding awareness.

Body Focus is a sensory awareness exercise for bringing conscious attention to the phenomena that are present in awareness. It is a process of checking into each of the physical senses, the quality of mind, and the emotions.

If you find your attention wandering during the body focus, be aware of that as well. Observe what you are experiencing and describe it as part of the flow. Then go back and finish working through your senses. You can be present with whatever is in your present experience; it may be a sense, a mood, or a state of mind. Once you start paying attention, everything you experience becomes informative, in a gentle, effortless way.

The meaning you experience at any moment may come just as much from the process of your awareness as from the content of your senses. Thus as you do the body focus, you may feel a shift, a settling perhaps, or even an activation. Your response isn't caused so much by what it is you are sensing. Rather it's from the process of becoming present with yourself.

Your senses are the lenses through which you make contact

with your world. Being aware of those lenses is the first step to consciously choosing what information you want to focus on. As you practice the body focus, you may find you spend all your time with one sense. You can also make a conscious choice to explore other senses to balance your awareness.

Describing

Each time you think of a word to describe what you are experiencing you alter your perceptions. Even if you have a perception of what you would clearly call red and you describe it as red, your perception is changed. You will then be seeing it differently. Your conscious mind is always translating the present through the filter of previous experiences. This is a natural part of the bridging that happens between the conscious and the unconscious, between ourselves and the object of our perceptions. There is no truly neutral description of anything we experience. You have learned to focus more on the associations you have than the actual experience you are having.

Your descriptions become more accurate as you learn to relax into what you are sensing, without rushing to describe or label it. With that relaxation, the words you use will come from the living present of your experience. If a word comes to mind that doesn't accurately describe what you are sensing, you will be more able to recognize that difference. When that happens, you can stay with your sensation until a more accurate or descriptive word emerges. Imagine that your experience is more important than the words you speak.

So, if you are perceiving a color, a texture, or a sound, let yourself enjoy it. Allow yourself to stay with it until words start to come. Even as words arise, stay with your sensing; your expression will lead you to the next words, the next sense, and the next unfolding of your consciousness. You may be surprised where the flow of language takes you in response to your perceptions.

Also, as you do these exercises, take the time to write legibly. Having a meaningful experience is only half the process; communicating, or bringing it back to normal consciousness makes it complete. Writing down your experiences helps you bridge different states of consciousness.

Every time you write, even in a slightly altered state of body focus, let yourself relax into your senses, trusting that the words will come. You can achieve a balance between being relaxed and allowing your experiences to flow on the one hand and communicating on the other. As you go further into experiences that are not directed by your conscious mind, you will be better able communicate what you are experiencing. Being able to communicate while you're having an experience frees you to enjoy the experience in the present and go deeper into it.

Chapter 3

*Perception is inherently participatory. To the body,
the world is not 'object'. There is no 'me' apart from
an 'other.' Everything is animate for the sensing body.
Touch a tree and the tree is touching you back.*
                              - David Abram [1]

Spontaneous Shifting States

Whenever you attend to and describe a perception or feeling you are experiencing, you are increasing your ability to shift in and out of different states of consciousness. You are building bridges in your mind and body so you can travel back and forth with ease. As I mentioned, you build a healthy flexibility in your mind and body. Being able to shift into your body and be with a feeling will help you relieve mental stress. It will also help you validate and release emotions you're carrying. You can communicate what is alive in you this way. You are making your mind/body system more responsive and healthy. It doesn't matter if you write, speak or gesture with your body; if you're expressing something of your living energy it will enliven you.

Here's a very simple bridging exercise to try:

The next time you find yourself daydreaming, enjoy it and

> *allow a part of yourself to observe your experience as it's happening.*
> *Then afterwards, write down what you remember.*

The challenge is to learn to allow daydreaming to happen while being aware. It's easy and, at the same time not so easy. Daydreaming is one place in most people's lives where the unconscious leads. It's enjoyable, natural, and familiar, yet it's truly an altered state led by the unconscious. Practicing this exercise can be a tremendous help in recognizing your intuitive information. If you try to be aware when you are daydreaming, you may first only catch yourself after you've returned. If so, then you can still track where you went. Can you remember when you shifted, or what stimulated the shift? With practice you will begin to sense yourself daydreaming as it's happening.

> **If you pay attention to your body, you will have more access to what is in your subconscious.**

You can do the same thing with sleeping dreams. When you become conscious after sleeping, stay with the sense of the dream as you remember it. At first it may seem like a delicate balance. As your conscious mind becomes activated, it may seem to chase your dream perceptions away. But with practice you can stay with the felt sense of the dream and the threads of memory, and write legibly and concisely what you remember. Then you can even go back into the dream again.

That ability starts now, in this moment, with the sensory exercises you've been doing. Can you allow a part of your awareness to stay in touch with the sounds you're hearing? As you read and hear simultaneously, you build your bridging ability. Other sounds or sensations, when they arise, can then be attended to and recognized.

If you pay attention to your body, you will have more access to what is in your subconscious. For example, your body tells you when you're hungry. Is that intuition? I would say so. It is a direct communication from your unconscious. You may not think of it as intuitive because it's so familiar. What other ways is your unconscious already communicating with you? Unconscious intelligence and energy pervades your being and flows through every channel of perception, every thought and feeling.

Most information received through sensory channels is processed unconsciously. Then it bubbles up to conscious awareness. It doesn't matter if the information is received intuitively or directly through the physical senses. When you are fully present with your perceptions, much more complex information becomes accessible.

If you were to eat an apple with your full sensory presence, your experience may become incredibly rich. That richness may be directly caused by the physical transfer of information through the sense organs, but there also may be intuitive information. For example, while chewing you may perceive an image of a place and a landscape that might be where the apple came from. With this image, you may also feel a sense of warmth and moisture indicating where it grew. Similarly, you might perceive how old the tree is, who picked the apple, or what they were feeling. The immediacy of sensory awareness takes you out of what you think and moves you into direct perceptions not limited by your conscious beliefs and thoughts. You connect with what is, beyond the limitations of your physical senses.

> *And, I suspect, while making no such claims for myself, a great deal of the world's most significant thinking has begun just like this, with the body, in the heart of the night, coming, for all I can tell, from a place so far within us that it is very likely common to all of us.*
> — David Brooks [7]

Fascination

It doesn't matter what channel of perception you focus on. When allowed to unfold, all channels of perception will take you into the realm of direct knowing. If you allow yourself to be fascinated, to enjoy what you are experiencing, your sensing will take you deeper.

How do you enjoy something?
Does it take will or effort?
Remember the feeling of enjoying or being fascinated by an experience.
Describe what that feels like.

How does remembering a pleasurable experience make you feel now?

How do you enjoy a hot bath? You fill the tub with water and perhaps light a candle. You set yourself up for the experience with conscious intent. But in order to get into the experience of the bath you have to let go of the preparation and the doing and get into it. At some point you have to let go and get in to what you have created.

How about a sunset? When evening comes, you can sit on the porch and watch the sunset happen all by itself. It takes no effort. In fact, when you release any idea of doing anything, then greater enjoyment and satisfaction comes. When you follow your fascination, you will naturally immerse into what you're sensing. A sunset may begin with an image, but quickly it blends into your other senses. The feeling on your skin becomes part of the equation, as does your breathing and other sounds or smells. Perhaps past memories or significant feelings surface as part of the present.

> **When you follow your fascination, you will naturally immerse into what you're sensing.**

As you allow this sensing, your conscious mind lets go. All these aspects combine, without effort, guided by your unconscious intelligence. (Remember the daydreaming exercise. You may start to daydream while you're watching the beauty in front of you.) As you allow your experience, your letting go may not be passive either. You may feel like moving or talking or engaging in some other creative release of energy.

Learning to allow and to let go is an integral part of coming to your senses, finding health and balance in your body, and developing intuition. Your deeper intelligence will always take you where you need to go if you allow it.

Sleep is a good example of the relationship between the conscious and unconscious. Can you make yourself fall asleep? No, not without ingesting a medication to help. Sleep is a process where the conscious mind lets go and surrenders to the unconscious intentions of the body. You may consciously want to sleep, but you only fall asleep when the conscious mind lets go.

Have you struggled to fall asleep? In our society so dominated by conscious control and will, sleep is one place where many people struggle to let go. Anything you can do to shift into a more receptive and open connection with your body and your senses will help you sleep. If you're having trouble sleeping, do the full body focus before you go to bed. Take your time. Sense and describe everything you are experiencing in all of the channels of awareness you can attend to.

Personal Validation

Being present with yourself is especially important if you are experiencing uncomfortable sensations or feelings. How often have you been wanting to sleep and rest, but found that your body was too tense or uncomfortable. Perhaps you realized that you were holding anxiety or anger in your body. The body focus will help you name and release even these uncomfortable sensations.

Here is another simple, yet profoundly valuable exercise you can use in conjunction with the body focus to help you release anything you're holding that is uncomfortable, awkward or fearful. I call this exercise the Personal Validation Process.

> *Sense and perceive what is alive in you. Then describe your thoughts, sensations and emotions to yourself. (Body Focus.)*
> *For anything you're experiencing that is uncomfortable to you, say to yourself, "I am feeling (describe what it is) and I'm OK." Speak those words into the feelings and sensations in your body, wherever you experience them.*

It can be helpful to describe your discomfort with sense words. For example, if you're feeling pain in your back, what color would it be? What sound would it have? Would it have a texture? Then use the words in the sentence above. Repeat that phrase several times. Speaking it softly with your breath.

Even if you don't believe that you're OK, try it. Saying you're OK doesn't mean you want it to continue. It means that as it's happening you're still here. You're still breathing, thinking and feeling. You are OK!

A helpful variation of this is to say, "I am (your words) and I'm OK", leaving out the word "feeling". Again, this may seem strange, but it helps you connect with the experience more directly, which is often what your unconscious mind does not want to do!

Then, if after repeating that phrase several times, you don't feel OK, or you don't believe you're OK, ask yourself, "What am I needing now? Whatever comes to mind, ask yourself, "If I had that, how would it make me feel?" That feeling or need becomes the focus for the next step.

Then take some deep relaxing breaths and tell yourself, "With each breath I am breathing, I am becoming (the feeling or need you're wanting)."

Lastly, if you need to actually do something to take care of yourself, do so!

This validation process can be incredibly effective for releasing whatever it is you're experiencing that you resist. If you're struggling to fall asleep, it will help you let go and come into your body in a safe, relaxing way. Often just saying "I'm OK" will start to shift you into a more comfortable and relaxed place. Using your senses and being with your feelings will take you out of your mind and allow your unconscious to guide you into sleep.

This Body Focus/Validation Process works just as effectively any time during the day when you are struggling or feeling uncomfortable. You can use it as a very effective means of self-soothing when you're stressed or anxious, calming yourself when you're angry, or even re-energizing yourself when you're tired.

If you do the body focus and you notice discomfort, you also have a perfect opportunity to validate the messages from your unconscious and incorporate the information you receive. Say you have a discomfort in your gut. You describe its color, texture, and shape. As you're describing it, you feel an emotion. A sadness comes or an anger. Staying with the flow, you comment to yourself on each piece saying, "I am.... and I'm OK." As you comment, you may feel a shift in the intensity of the sensations in your body. You may also have emotions that arise. A release of emotion may be what your unconscious was wanting or needing all along. Think of it as a rebalancing of energy in your mind/body system.

When you respond to these signals with conscious attention, you may gain insight or awareness of an action you need to take for your health and well-being. If so, be sure to respond to that information. When you get in the practice of attending to the messages of your unconscious, the communication becomes more direct and clear. Perhaps the next time you won't need to become so uncomfortable to hear its solicitations.

Conversely, there may be many times when there is no conscious awareness why a sensation or a feeling comes into your body, heart or mind. It may be that just being present with yourself, validating and releasing is all the meaningfulness you need. In the same way you wonder or marvel at a sunset, you can let a discomfort or irritation move through you. If it has more meaning that you need to know, you will find out in another session. Your body is the perfect vehicle for the expression of your unconscious.

> *What the body is moved by are energies that it does not control. These are the energies that control the body. They come in from the great biological ground, whatever it may be. They are there. They are energies and they are manners of consciousness.*
>
> *- Joseph Campbell* [8]

Coming out of your mind and into your sensing, living body can unlock the wisdom of your whole being. When you awaken in the morning after sleeping, your letting go moves you against gravity, into an upright position. Think of dancing. In the joy of the moment there is no resistance to body movements. Dancing becomes more enjoyable the more you allow a spontaneous flow of movement. When your movement is aligned with your whole being, letting go can become even more active than you've experienced before.

What is your body telling you now?
Is there something you could be allowing to happen?
Then let it happen!

Many of us have had some form of intuitive experience at some point in our lives. One of the most common experiences is having a strong sense or feeling relating to something happening in our lives. For instance, you may be contemplating a new job, a new relationship, or a new travel experience. You may have a strong sense or feeling supporting your intention, or you may suddenly sense foreboding. You may pay attention to the information or not.

Whatever your response, the memory of that event stays with you. You may be intrigued, puzzled, or even changed in some way. You may consequently have similar experiences at other times. These experiences may not fit in with the logic and sensibility of the rest of your life, but in some way you find them valuable. There is a quality to them that is compelling. One intuitive experience can stay with you for years and have life-changing effects.

Whether or not you consider your intuitive experiences deeply meaningful or exceptional, they may have subtly transformed your perception of reality. Perhaps they led you to exploring intuition and reading this book. If you follow the lead of your intuitive body, you will approach the edge between what you can know in your mind and what you can perceive through direct experience. How much you learn may directly relate to how much time you spend extending your consciousness out to the edges of your experience.

Experiences at the Edge

Experiences at these edge territories have a quality that is compelling, captivating, and sometimes bewildering. But we sense they are valuable; that is partly why they linger. The conscious mind struggles with them though, not being able to put them into a neat box. Specific conscious understandings do come with experience and familiarity. Paths can be mapped. With familiarity, experiences gained at those edge territories can be trusted.

When I was a young man, just out of high school, I was attempting to expand my consciousness with hallucinogens, meditation, and yoga. One evening, following an altered state experience, I decided I wanted to telepathically communicate with my brother Matthew. I crept up the stairs and sat outside the closed door to his room. I could easily hear him playing his electric guitar through the door. I focused all my energies, willing him to become aware of my presence. I said his name inside my head many times. I commanded him to notice me but nothing happened. I started to get tired. Then I started listening to the music he was playing. I liked it. I fell into the music and lost my sense of sitting by the door.

In the midst of this flowing music the door jerked open and Matthew stared down at me. "Ah ha!" he said. I was just as surprised as he was. I asked him what happened. He said that while he was playing he became aware of the door to his room; his attention had been drawn there. He said he put down his guitar, stood up, walked over to the door and jerked it open. He had sensed me. My experiment worked. Logically, I figure he could have sensed me by registering the sounds I made coming up the stairs. Was it "true" telepathy? I don't know. I do know that it was an energetic, meaningful experience for both of us.

One thing that has always fascinated me about this experiment was what I experienced. I basically let go of my desire and found myself flowing into the music. When Matthew stopped playing and came to the door, the music I was hearing didn't stop. I had melted into the music and stayed there until I was jarred out of it by the door opening.

I now believe my experiment was successful because of my strong intention followed by my letting go and forgetting it. This is true with all of my experiences at these edge territories. There is a relationship between the known and the unknown at the edge of our conscious awareness.

When you perceived the picture on page 25, there were responses in other, unconscious parts of your being. The image may have activated memories, feelings, and even physical sensations. It may still be stirring you in a subtle way.

The unconscious aspects of ourselves are fundamental to who we are; they provide the ground on which our personality and our sense of self reside. Intuition, creativity, wisdom, and spiritual awareness come into our consciousness through the unconscious.

In this book, I use the term unconscious to refer to the vehicle through which these abilities come into our consciousness, and I tend to refer to the source as the Larger Self or Higher Self. You can approach that guide in whatever way is meaningful to you and fits your beliefs. Regardless of what framework you use, psychic functioning, intuition, creativity, soul-knowing and spirit are accessible to you. Developing intuition can help you develop your transpersonal and spiritual parts.

Practically speaking, with intuition, you can know who's calling on the telephone before you answer. When your car breaks down, you can discern if it is something simple you can fix before you call a tow truck. You may even be able to tell the mechanic what to look for. You can protect yourself and change your course of action, when you pay attention to a feeling of danger before you walk down a certain street or get into a car with a stranger. You can find lost objects, animals or people. You can make life transitions easier by gaining a different perspective or a clearer sense of your life purpose. You can ask a question inwardly about your body or health and receive a clear image of what action you need to take. You can start to validate your ability to know and trust yourself. The self that you learn to trust is much larger than your conscious mind.

Perhaps even more importantly, you can move into a way of being that feels more congruent, healthy and alive. Charlotte Selver [30], who was a pioneer in work on sensory awareness, described how we could remember and reawaken a sense of wonder and awe in the living of the present moment. She also suggested that when we come into a subtle connection with our senses and our living bodies, we can achieve a higher level of functioning and tap into our innate abilities for healing, renewal and balancing.

Exploring intuition is one way to recover these innate capacities and to restore our health and well being. Being open and receptive at a threshold and noticing what you sense starts the process. Trusting your response, even if it's not rational, is the next step. You can open the door to larger parts of yourself.

Can you imagine having an intimate understanding of intuition that is entirely formed by your own experience?

Having practical intuitive experiences where you get feedback can help your learning. In the following pages we will dive further into practical ways to learn to use intuition. Your inner awareness can lead you to useful applications in every day life.

Chapter 4

Imagining and Perceiving

Now you can experience letting go in the present. If I asked you to imagine a color, what would you experience? Close your eyes and try it. Ask yourself:

"What color now?"
It's just your imagination, nothing difficult. Try it.
Notice what happens.
Describe what you experience.

If you are primarily a visual person, you may spontaneously perceive a color. If you're not primarily a visual person then imagining a color may be difficult. Be patient with yourself. Give your sensing a few moments to resolve.

Now use your sense of smell.
"What do you smell now?"
Consciously breathe a moment; allow yourself to imagine an odor.
Describe your experience.

What do you perceive? When it's your imagination, it requires little or no effort. It can be playful. Like falling asleep or enjoying a bath, there is a part of you that knows how to play in this way. If it feels awkward for you, tell yourself, "It's awkward, and I'm OK!" and enjoy it. When you imagine, it doesn't matter what comes up, there's no right or wrong. There's no one telling you what you should get or how to qualify what comes up.

> *Can you imagine a name now?*
> *What comes to mind first?*

Imagining allows you to relax conscious control. It brings up a creative energy from inside you that is spontaneous. Imagining allows you to extend an awareness that isn't analytically directed. Each time I ask you, "Can you imagine..." and you respond, you are activating a non-analytical awareness. Anything you read here can activate your imagination. In your imagination one plus two may not always equal three. Instead,

"Imagine..." plus "a color" may equal ∞
(Here ∞ represents a form of meaning that is outside logic thinking.)

Imagining opens a door for the living presence of your deeper self to enter your awareness.

> *Imagine you can invite a larger part of your being into your awareness.*

When you open up your awareness with imagination, you access your unrestricted, free-flowing creative energy. Just as easily as you can imagine a color, you can learn to allow instant response to other intentions that aren't conscious. You can learn to let go and allow these other parts to guide you.

Imagination and intuition are similar in that information is experienced inwardly. There is no objective verification for them, at least not initially. But there is an important difference between imagination and intuition.

Imagination is an active extension of conscious will into our inner creative space. When we imagine a color, we may pick one that is floating on the surface of the mind. The mind says, "OK, I just saw the color blue next to me, so now I am 'imagining' blue." Then we see blue clearly. When we imagine, the unconscious responds creatively, but the conscious mind is still involved. When we imagine something we create it. We formulate it from possibilities, potentials, and from the full range of our previous experiences. This is an amazing ability; it allows us to expand creatively into new, unexperienced territories.

When we imagine, our whole being responds—body, mind, heart and spirit. Our experience then feeds back into what we are imagining and our experience becomes stronger. Imagination allows us to experience things before they actually happen, to try out new possibilities, and to get a sense what we want or don't want to do. But this imagining is still based on our previous experience. It's difficult to imagine something we've never experienced before.

When you open up your awareness with imagination, you access your unrestricted, free-flowing creative energy.

The same is true even with perceptions of our physical senses. What we experience is shaped by our mental associations and memories. Even though we may be perceiving something real and physical, we often see it through the filters of our previous experience. When this happens we are partially perceiving the image or the memory of the physical object, rather than the object itself. These perceptions and memories are obstacles to intuitive perception. Any time the mind comes in and labels or quantifies what we are perceiving, then we cease direct perception and the receiving of new information.

When we quiet our will—our active, intentional mind—we move closer to direct perception. This is what sensory awareness training facilitates. Intuition is direct perception. The intuitive process starts with some form of intention and perception follows when we let go of any conscious direction.

For example, I want to perceive a plant sitting on my desk. At the moment of intent, I already "know" what this plant is. I have numerous experiences of this plant, from watering it, looking at it, touching it, and moving it around on my desk. But when I let go of my image and start to sense what is there, I shift from knowing to experiencing. Some of my perceptions may coincide with what I already know. But if I stay attentive, I will experience a new richness of sensation that is more than my memories and images of this plant.

When we become receptive to what we are actually perceiving with our senses, we enter into a whole new world of discovery. The every day world becomes fascinating again. When we quiet the mind and become receptive to inner awareness, we discover intuitive knowing, an aliveness and engagement with the phenomenal world.

Intuitive awareness occurs in exactly the same way your imagination uses, through senses, feelings, and thoughts. The only difference is that you aren't directing or controlling what comes into your awareness. When you have an intent, to perceive a color for instance, the intent starts the process. Then when you relax your mind and will, a spontaneous color arrives, maybe a color that you've never encountered before.

One way to notice the difference between imagination and intuition is to pay attention to the quality of your inner perceptions. What you imagine tends to be clearer, slower moving, and easier to grasp. It is held by conscious will and memory.

Take a moment and imagine a rose...
Engage your senses with your memory of a rose.
How do you experience it?
Which senses come easy?
Describe these senses.

When you imagine a rose, you can hold it in your awareness. If you are a visual person, then you will see the color and shape in your mind's eye. If your sense of smell is strong, the experience of the smell will stay with you. These senses you imagine tend to be stable.

Direct perception and intuition, however, are more fluid and changeable. When you shift to direct perception, energy, information and physical energy flow and change constantly. When I observe the plant on my desk, my eyes shift rapidly, taking in many different types of information—colors, shapes, and textures. When I hold on to one perception, the flow stops. If I'm not staying present, my sensing turns into an image and a memory and then becomes more static.

You can trust direct perception. It flows and changes, constantly remaining meaningful or useful. The meaning we experience when we become immersed in a bath or a sunset comes from that flow. Being in the flow can be a tremendously valuable experience. When I am in that flow, a quality I perceive from my plant may trigger a feeling or an insight in me. If I am viewing that plant with an openness to deeper meaning, my perception of the plant would become more intuitive. My initial intention to perceive intuitively opens me to new intuitive information. I do not stay in my mind with my conscious understanding of the label, plant.

When I perceive my plant, I might be curious to know if it needs water. Then as I relax into the plant experience—the colors, textures, and energies—I might gradually become aware of thirst in my body. I might feel thirst as part of all the rest of the richness of the plant that I'm experiencing. I may also realize that my thirst is connected to the plant.

Throughout this book I'll offer opportunities to activate inner awareness either with or without conscious will. Inner awareness with will becomes imagination; without will it is intuition. Both awarenesses are very useful. Imagination engages your creativity with what you already know. Any change is guided by your inner creativity, by the unconscious mind. Imagination establishes a new awareness of things and makes them concrete within you. From imagination you can shift to direct perception.

Direct Perception

Here's an exercise to facilitate this shift. Have a pen, some crayons or markers and paper handy. You can read through this and then do it on your own.

> *Close your eyes. Inhale deeply. Then purse your lips like you're blowing through a straw and exhale all the way out until you're comfortably empty.*
> *Repeat this breath several times.*
> *Let your breath return to a comfortable rhythm.*
> *Imagine what it feels like to come into the warm sun when your body is cold. (If for some reason the sun doesn't feel safe to you, remember a hot bath or another enjoyable experience.)*
> *Remember that warmth and feel it on your skin.*
> *Remember what it feels like when your body relaxes.*
> *Remember how good it feels.*
> *Take a few moments and enjoy these feelings.*
> *Enjoy your body relaxing.*
> *Remember how your body moves differently when you relax.*
> *Experience the "letting go" movement of muscles releasing.*
>
> *Do it now.*
>
> *Once you experience some comfortable relaxation in your body, allow that specific memory to fade.*
> *Let your senses settle into a comfortable, quiet place in the present.*
>
> *Then say to yourself,*
> *"I would like to perceive a color from an intuitive source."*
> *Then let go of that thought.*
> *Relax and allow whatever comes into your awareness, through any channel.*
>
> *There's no hurry.*
> *Just be aware and be patient with yourself.*
> *You may have an immediate response, or it may take a little longer.*
> *Staying relaxed, you can pay attention.*

Notice what you perceive.
You don't have to do anything.
Just observe whatever happens in your whole being.

Then try a couple other senses—odors, textures, or sounds.
Say to yourself, "I would like to perceive..."

Enjoy the spontaneous perceptions that arise.

Do it now.

Afterwards, describe your perceptions and experience as best as you can.
Can you describe without labeling?
Even if your response is only a feeling or a thought, you can describe it.
There is no wrong response. Just be aware and describe.
Don't censor yourself.
If you perceive colors, draw them on your paper.
Use a crayon or marker that's close to that color.
Drawing connects you to nonverbal ways of processing.
Enjoy the experience of describing and drawing as well.
Take your time.

Do it now.

Afterwards, I'd like you to look at whatever you wrote. Is it possible to imagine that there truly are no wrong responses here? What's important is that you open your intention to receiving intuitive information, and then allow whatever comes. For example, if you didn't get any visual response to your first intention to perceive a color, that's OK. What did happen? Did you have thoughts, feelings, or perhaps some other inner body sensation? If so, then you could simply describe those things, since they were your response. That way you start validating whatever your unconscious is presenting to you.

The perceptions or experiences you had may have no meaning

to you. That's OK too. A sensation that you experienced also may be meaningful to you in some way. If so, then describe that meaning as part of your process. There is a form of therapy that uses colors to heal. Many people perceive colors having a vibrational quality that affects our bodies and minds. Letting your unconscious guide the choice of color can be informative and even healing. If you want to explore color, spend a little time imagining that color and holding it in your awareness. See how it makes you feel. Take notes!

On the other hand, your color may mean nothing. That's OK too. As you slow down and explore with your inner sensing, you open the door to more meaning. I encourage you to do this exercise again, allowing whatever comes and learn how to let go and allow.

When you allow yourself to perceive inwardly, without conscious control, you move into the flow of intuition and information appears. Intuition is usually more subtle than imagination. You can learn to allows its presence in your awareness as intimately and directly as your own inner thoughts and feelings.

Imagine again that you can open to a flow of intuitive information and awareness that is already inside you. Imagine you can perceive something directly.

When you imagine your intuitive sense, you may notice a feeling that comes into your body or a shift in your state of mind. Wherever imagining takes you, enjoy the process and learn about yourself.

Allow your intuitive sense to be with you now as you are reading.

Chapter 5

You've opened the door to your sensing and imagining. The more you engage your attention and awareness with the body of your living experience, the more you will be able to keep a healthy balance in your mind and body and access your intuition. This engagement takes a different kind of effort than our work with our usual, focused, analytical consciousness. You engage with intuition by allowing rather than striving.

> *Take another slow, deep breath.*
> *Enjoy the feeling of being present.*
> *Can you allow the sensation of your body to be with you as you read?*

By occasionally connecting with your breath or your body, your mental experience will be more balanced with your physical and emotional awareness. Each time you connect with the body of your experience you open your awareness to different ways of knowing.

> *Pause, and listen to what you're hearing.*
> *As you relax into what you're hearing, then let language come.*
> *Describe those sounds to yourself.*

As your attention shifts back to reading, the sounds around you may recede again into the background. This is a natural process as your focus shifts to this channel of awareness. All the channels are still being attended to and processed at an unconscious level. When there is information that needs your attention, your subconscious will bring it to your attention. With attention, you can cultivate a rich partnership between your conscious and unconscious. You may even sense how that is already happening.

Softening the Conscious Mind

When you pause and listen to sounds, feel the sensations in your body. When you enjoy the quality of light you're perceiving, you shift your awareness into a more passive and receptive mode. In these sensory experiences you are more open to other kinds of information and sensing. When you read an affirmation or a suggestion in this text, take a deeper breath. Allow a shifting into a softer, more receptive awareness. You might focus on hearing the sounds of the words, as if you are speaking them to yourself. Try to hear your voice as you read these words:

> *Your inner sensation can become a larger part of your present experience.*
> *Bring to mind a feeling or a memory you enjoy.*
> *As you remember the sensation, allow your body to respond.*

Focusing on the sounds of the words or a pleasant sensation in your body while you're reading, softens your eyes and your sense of "I". When you soften your eyes and the muscles around your eyes, your will and your sense of doing softens. Then you become more able to perceive deeper meanings and insights. Your perception allows more depth into your awareness. In this way your senses can be the stimulus for greater movements in your whole being.

As with the outer senses, when you soften your mind and body, your inner doors of perception also become more open. A pleasant, intentional thought can help to soften your inner awareness:

Imagine your eyes softening as you continue reading.

Inside you is a deeper part that can see the larger picture. You may call it the higher self, your unconscious, spirit, or God. That inner presence may also remain unnamed. It knows who you are, what you're about, and where you're going in your life. It knows how each experience moves you towards your life's purpose. It guides you each moment, with every breath and every thought.
You can be more aware of that larger part of you, even now, as you are reading. That part of you resonates with all the other times when you felt you were "on track", resonating with the meaning and purpose of your life.

You might remember a special moment in your life when a deeply meaningful feeling opened for you.
Where were you?
What was happening around you?
What was happening inside you?
Take a moment and breathe into that memory.
Enjoy that felt sense.
Allow it to be with you.

Those memories are still embedded in your being. A part of your being always is attuned to your deeper self.

Notice how it feels to welcome that felt sense of well-being and connection. Enjoy that feeling. As you continue reading and exploring, allow that awareness to spread out into your next moments and your next unfolding.

Extend that feeling longer if you wish, without reading.
Take your time.
Absorb these feelings.

Then, if you wish, when you are ready, take notes, draw and describe your experience.

With each suggestion in this text, you have the opportunity to shift into a more receptive state of mind. Your unconscious responds to what suits you and discards the rest.

I first encountered this idea of word activation while learning about hypnosis. While reading some talks by Milton Erickson [15], a respected medical hypnotist, a part of me entered a hypnotic state. Only when I paused in my reading, did I realize my senses had sharpened, my breathing had deepened, and my whole body had relaxed. In this open, receptive state, I easily understood the trance experience Erickson was talking about. I was fascinated by my awareness changes.

We automatically enter a trance-like state when we focus on something that interests us. Our awareness engages with the words or senses and we become more attuned, focused and entranced. Erickson used this understanding of trance awareness in his speech so that people hearing him talk, (and later, his readers) could experience a deeper, inner connection to his words from within their own trance awareness.

You can notice if and when this happens to you while you're reading this book. When you encounter a word or idea you enjoy, you might sense a shift in your body or your attention. Your attention may wander for a moment. You may also sense a shift to a calmer or more relaxed state. When that happens, pause a moment and recognize it. You can let it remain in your awareness.

> *You can attend to subtle shifts and perceptions when they occur.*

Attending to your process builds a bridge between willing and allowing, between the conscious and the unconscious. That bridge leads to intuition.

> *Even now, there is an inner ally leading you.*
> *Can you sense it?*
> *Can you imagine it?*
> *It is an ally you can trust, leading you to your next insight or understanding.*

This easy learning arises from within you.
It is easy and natural.

Whatever you encounter, even if it's a perception or sensation you've never recognized before, you can be aware of it, sense it, and then describe it. With an unknown, or a never-before experienced sensation, no previous mental images get in the way. Giving yourself permission to bask in these unlabeled areas in your awareness draws out your deeper intelligence and wisdom. Something other than what is contained in your conscious mind becomes meaningful to you.

Spatial Body Focus

Now I would like to use a more spatial way to go through the body focus. Below is the graphic I used earlier to represent the channels through which we perceive information.

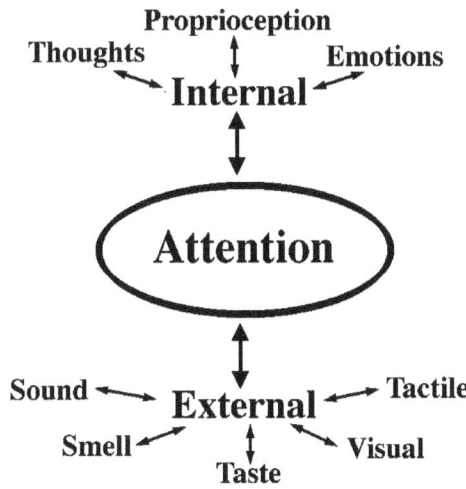

Figure 3

This time, as you go through the body focus, place each of the words that describe your experience in its place around the center as in the figure above. This spatial relationship will also engage your brain in a different way. Start closer in to the center with the channels that are immediately present. Then work your way outwards as you explore the other channels that aren't as dominant. Here's an example of how the body focus works for me in this moment:

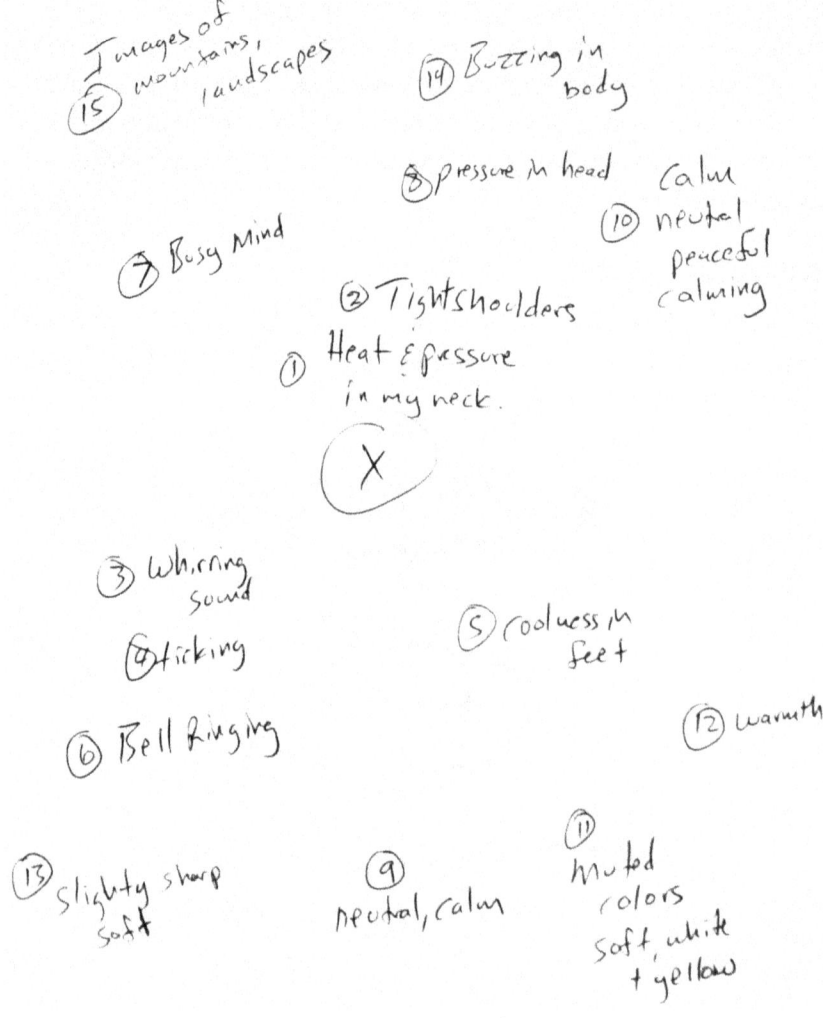

Figure 4 - Spatial Body Process

I numbered my perceptions to show how the process went for me. I started in the center with an "X", then worked outward placing my perceptions where they fit into the map. You can see that what was dominant to begin with were some inner body sensations of discomfort in my neck and shoulder. Sounds were next, and I went on from there. I had to consciously check in with smells and tastes later on in the process to see what was there, since those channels weren't very active. Finally, I started to get some internal imagery showing up, similar to dream images of mountains and landscapes.

> *Take a few moments now and go through the body focus process again.*
> *Start with what's alive and active in you.*
> *Place each perception on your own map.*
> *Be sure to check in with each of your channels of perception and attend to what you are perceiving, even if it's subtle.*
>
> *Check out your emotional and mental states and any interior perceptions or sensations you are having in your body.*
> *Take your time.*
> *When you're finished, be aware how the process affected you.*
> *Describe that change as well.*

For those of you who are spatially oriented, you may find it enjoyable to allow this kind of flow into your process. You may also shift where you put different channels on your map. Once you have it established, you can use the map to stimulate your awareness. For example, if you're not aware of any smells, then just by placing the tip of your pen on the paper in the smell area and waiting, can help you bring that channel more into your awareness.

Baseline

With each body focus, you will start to see similarities in your descriptions. You may discover that your first "check-in" tends to focus on one particular sense. Also, some quality or feeling you are having may be similar each time you check in. These similarities will reveal where you spend your time; they are feelings or sensations that are dominant in your day-to-day life. Whatever regularly shows up in your body focus is your baseline.

The baseline is different for everyone and is a result of what we've decided is important to us. Granted, you are changing all the time, and shifting in and out of different experiences, sensations and feelings. Underneath all of that, you have your basic sense of self. For me, as in my last illustration, feelings of calm, neutrality and peace will often show up, especially, after I've "cleared" the stronger sensations and perceptions. Knowing your own baseline makes it easier to recognize changes that occur in you.

When you do the body focus, you may begin feeling edgy or more peaceful. Perhaps your vision becomes more sharp. These changes may not mean anything at first, but as you stay present with yourself more meaning may come. For example, you may feel a peacefulness. You enjoy it. As you experience it again you begin to see a connection between that feeling and some outer stimulus. You might begin to notice how that feeling precedes talking with someone you know. That understanding is intuitive.

> **Baseline** is the general constellation of senses, feelings, and thoughts that make up your normal state of consciousness.

Another possibility is that your mind may see no correlation to that peaceful feeling. Yet, if it makes you pause, take a deep breath and relax, that may be a very important meaning.

Beliefs.

Why are you reading this book?
Do you expect an experience or some kind of information?
Take a moment and reflect on this question.
Then write down your responses.

As you come into your sensory body in a healthy, fluid way and open the door to your intuition, your sense of who you are and what you are will expand and change. As this happens, your personal expectations and beliefs also will come more to the surface. If you engage yourself fully with each new idea and each new experience, your personal beliefs will be stretched. You will understand more clearly what your beliefs are. The beliefs and attitudes you bring to learning about intuition are important.

I've come up with some questions to help you be more conscious of your attitudes and beliefs relating to intuition and consciousness. Take time to answer these questions thoroughly; elaborate on your answers. The more clearly and concisely you answer these questions, the more you will understand what beliefs you hold. You will have more freedom to choose which beliefs serve you and which ones you might want to change.

What is intuition?
Are you intuitive? If so, how?
Is intuition something you were (or were not) born with?
Why is it important for you to develop intuition or other extended capacities?
Are there any dangers involved with learning or using these abilities?
Are there limits to what you can do with these abilities?
If so, who or what sets these limits?
Do you have any moral obligations or guidelines to consider when using your intuition or other extended abilities?
Does the condition of your physical body or your mind affect your psychic abilities? Vice Versa?
Do you believe in a Higher Power, God, Great Spirit, or Spiritual Force? If so, how would you describe it?
Do you believe in guides, angels, spirits, or other non-physical teachers/protectors?
Do you have any protectors or guides?
Is it safe for you to trust your unconscious mind?
Is it safe for you to trust your higher consciousness?
Do you use your imagination? If so, how?
If you start learning to use intuition now, how or when would you know that you had more or improved abilities?

Take your time and answer each of these questions.

Considering and answering these questions will bring your

beliefs closer to conscious awareness. You have acquired beliefs through the course of your life, from your family, friends, or others who influenced you. Watching television or reading books probably also had an impact. Significant personal experiences certainly influenced your beliefs. These beliefs that are part of your being, determine how you experience the world, intuition, and your own awareness. These beliefs are important because they provide you with a framework to experience yourself and your intuition.

Becoming conscious of your beliefs is an essential part of making your intuitive abilities more accessible. As you continue exploring your intuition you will stretch your sense of who you are. With increasing awareness, you can choose more consciously how you respond to new information and experiences.

> *The limits of our mind are beliefs to be explored, not facts to be assumed.*
> *- John Lilly*

For now, you can let your beliefs rest. You will revisit them later, after exploring more with your awareness, your states of mind, and your intuition.

Sensory Awareness

Heightening and refining your awareness of normal sensory processes has a profound effect: you will become more aware of the wholeness of your self in every moment. When you connect with your sensory being, you become more awake and alert and immersed in the richness of present-moment experience. Your mind naturally becomes calmer and more relaxed. You can also connect directly to what is sacred to you through your present-moment experiences.

Charlotte Selver was a pioneer in the use of sensory awareness as a practice to expand consciousness. She felt that the calmness of mind that comes with a sensory awareness practice leads to a fuller consciousness, where our own innate abilities at higher-level cognition and even intuition become accessible. In "A Report on Work in Sensory Awareness and Total Functioning" [30] she wrote:

*Full sensory connection with yourself can be profound.
A smell, taste or other bodily sensation can be a catalyst
for an experience of being larger than, or more than our
normal selves. Spiritual transformation can be realized
in physical sensory experience.*

The philosopher Christian de Quincey suggests the most direct way to God or a higher level experience is through the sensory engagement with the day-to day world.

*The way to meaning is reconnecting with the world of
nature through exuberant participation or through the
stillness of meditation, just being present and listening.*
12

You can experience God, spirit, or your sacred nature in this present moment, through the aliveness of your sensory being. This is a wonderful "side effect" to developing sensory awareness and intuition. You will know your life is meaningful and sacred. In a moment of sensing clearly, being connected to yourself in mind and body, you may have an "Aha" experience that reminds you how large you really are.

*Is it possible to invite a connection to a larger presence into
  this moment?
What if connection were to begin with this breath?*

If you go into your breath and let go, you may be drawn elsewhere. If your attention wanders while reading, notice it. Watch where it leads you. When your mind wanders, your unconscious is leading you somewhere else. There may be an opening into something more meaningful than where you are now. A word or phrase you read may trigger a memory, and then a forgotten feeling may rise to the surface. Whenever something arrives in your awareness, you can attend to its message.

*A wandering mind is an unconscious attempt to alter a
particular state.*
                                                    - Arnold Mindell 24

Meaning may be communicated to your awareness through the languages of the body, the spirit, or other natural channels. These are the communications from non-conscious parts of you and are directed by your deep self, higher self, or spirit. Recognizing and validating them brings them more and more into your life.

What are you sensing now?
Are you experiencing other channels of communication?
Pay attention.
Take notes.
And by all means, respond if necessary.

Chapter 6

If you consider entering into a sensory, intuitive dialogue with something, you open the door not only to previously unknown information, but also to your transformation. Rumi expresses the reflective nature of this kind of dialogue in one of his poems:

> *I sit in front of him in silence,*
> *and set up a ladder made of patience,*
> *and if in his presence a language from beyond joy*
> *and beyond grief begins to pour from my chest,*
> *I know that his soul is as deep and bright*
> *as the star Canopus rising over Yemen.*
> *And so when I start speaking a powerful right arm*
> *of words sweeping down, I know him from what I say,*
> *and how I say it, because there's a window open*
> *between us, mixing the night air of our beings.*
>   - *Translation by Coleman Barks* [4]

In the living, sensory present, we know ourselves through the phenomena we are experiencing. As in Rumi's example, the meaningfulness of an intuitive experience may come more from being in a flowing connection with something larger, than from the specific information we gather or the words we say. In that flow we realize an awareness of self that is larger than any specific content.

Sense an Object

Thinking about merging and allowing the flow of awareness, we'll explore more sensing. Read through this exercise before doing it.

Find an interesting object wherever you are. Think and feel the word interesting and observe what catches your attention. An object from the natural world might work well. Choose whatever suits you.

When you've decided on an object, try these suggestions:

Sit with it and allow yourself to sense it fully.
Focus on one sense at a time.
Engage your awareness with your object.

Touch it.
Move it.
Taste and smell it with all your attention.
Listen to the sounds your touch makes.
Notice the detail in each sense.

Take your time.
Enjoy what you experience.
Let yourself go deeper into each sense.
Give yourself time in each sense.

As you focus, you will likely perceive more detail than you normally do. Your sensing will open up and become richer and more interesting. When this happens, do the following;

Stay with what you're experiencing and begin to describe your perceptions.
Be specific.
Be sure to use words that describe rather than label.
Work your way through all of your senses in this way.
Write down all your perceptions.

Chapter 6

Take your time.
Allow the right words to come.

For example, when I look for an object to describe, my eyes land on an object that sits on my desk. I start with visual impressions:

> *Soft reddish color, fading to lighter at the bottom, speckled surface, small black holes, a blue/gray swath of color across the middle. It's dark on one side, brighter on the other. It's angled on the sides, smaller at the top with slightly curved edges. It feels cold and hard, smoother on the back than the front, and fairly heavy, more so at the bottom.*
> *As I sense it, I notice a light, happy feeling coming up.*

What is your response to reading my description? Are you in a different state than if I were to just tell you it's a stone?

As you go through the sensing of your object be aware of other responses or changes in you, even if they don't seem related. Anything that occurs in you is part of the process.

> *As soon as I focus on my stone, I feel lighter inside—my energy, my fascination increases. There's a slight tightening in my forehead and a heaviness in my chest.*

Similar changes may happen to you. More will happen if you allow it. Sensing, you are in process. Just be aware of everything you experience. You can let your awareness remain with a new feeling until descriptions arise. Your sensations will evolve in a describable way.

Be aware, be present, and describe your way through the entire experience. When you shift your attention from your object back to reading, you can still be present.

Do the exercise now.

After sensing this way, you may find your senses or awareness altered. Did you describe that too? Focusing deeply into your senses may shift your mind into a trance, as if you were doing a meditation. If you enjoy that trance, you can do it more.

What surprised you about this sensing exercise?
What was challenging?
What happened in your mind while you were perceiving?
In your body? Your heart?

You can continue the exploration of this object as long as you want. You may even perceive intuitive information about it. If you think you are perceiving something intuitively, then get feedback. Ask someone who might know more about it. Remember, you are already intuitive and perceiving much more than your conscious mind can imagine.

Drawing

Drawing is a direct way to communicate that doesn't utilize the language processing centers of the brain. Thus, drawing can be less influenced by mental labels. It doesn't matter if you think you can draw or not; your experience is what is important.

You can do an exercise to deepen your receptive awareness. Find a magazine with pictures of people or animals. Magazines with advertising work well. Find a picture that interests you. Tear it out and place a piece of tracing paper or a thin blank paper over it. You should be able to see at least a few basic shapes through the paper. Rotate the picture and paper 180 degrees so the image is upside down. Looking through the blank paper, let your eyes follow any shapes, lines or contrasts you see. Trace with your pen what you see with your eyes. As you draw, enjoy the connection between seeing and drawing. It can be very relaxing to let your eyes and pen flow this way.

In order to trace what you see, you have to shift to a receptive awareness. Again, it doesn't matter what the result is; it's the process that's important. Enjoy the feeling of tracing and let it guide you. Notice how a shape can be just a shape without any meaning attached. As you trace, you may remember other times you felt this way. Enjoy that too.

> *You may even let go of thinking altogether.*
> *Do your tracing now.*

> *When you're done, leave the paper as it is upside-down.*

> *Describe what you are experiencing.*

Slide the picture out from under your drawing and turn it over so you can't see it. Look again at your drawing as it's still upside-down. Notice the shapes you've drawn. Is it possible to see it complete as it is, without needing to reorient it?

> *Imagine that.*

> *What does it feel like to let it be as it is?*
> *Describe that feeling.*

> *Is it possible to imagine that your drawing is an accurate representation of what you were experiencing?*

As you traced, you shifted into a more receptive and passive awareness. What you see now is a communication of that process. Allow that feeling to stay with you. If you see any value in the way you are feeling, then take note of it. You don't need to judge your drawing to determine if this experience had value for you.

> *Would it be OK to enjoy how you feel now, regardless what that image looks like when it's turned around?*

> *You can entertain the idea of validating and trusting your inner experience.*

You can turn the page around if you wish. Tracings and drawings done this way often turn out looking better than we thought they would. Rotating the image for the drawing helps bypass our stored images. Then we draw more from our direct perception. That is why this exercise is important for developing intuition. Any time you can shift from what you "know" into what you are actually perceiving, your communication will be clearer. This is especially true with inner intuitive awareness.

When you draw, unconscious information doesn't come through the language areas of the brain. Any time you have a feeling or sense you can't describe, drawing it will help that sense become conscious. The drawing may not look like anything specific to the conscious, analytical mind. That's OK. It still offers another way for meaning to emerge.

Drawing an Object

Now we'll take this medium of expression a step further. I'd like you to let your eye follow some of the shapes, contrasts, or colors of the object you described in the earlier exercise. As you follow it with your eye, let your pen draw that shape on the paper. You can do this even if you feel you're not artistic. Just pick a shape, a line or a texture and communicate what you perceive with your pen. Don't try to draw the whole object, just the parts that grab your attention. For example, if I were perceiving a telephone on my desk, I might put down some of these shapes:

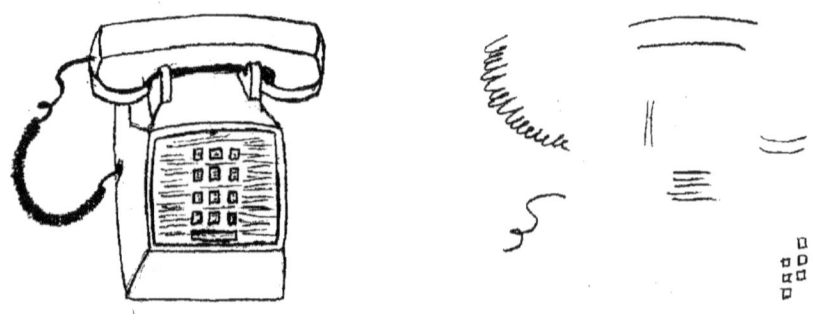

Figure 5

You can draw the elements of your object.

As you draw, imagine you're just tracing as you were through the tracing paper.
Let your eyes follow the lines you see.
Stay with the feeling and sensation of what you're seeing.
It doesn't matter how accurately you draw them, or even if they're in the right position.
By drawing, you build another bridge to your direct experience.

Enjoy the visual connection.
Draw some of the shapes of your object.

Do it now.

When you're finished, let the shapes be as they are.
Can you imagine that the shapes on the paper don't have to mean anything?

How did it feel to do that drawing exercise?
Describe your feelings.

When you let go of the need to know what you are drawing, your perceptions will come through more clearly. Starting with basic shapes, you create an ability to communicate your intuitive perceptions non-verbally. If you practice drawing shapes, colors, textures and feelings, you will be able to communicate more of your perceptions.

Pause and Remember...

You can remember and revisit things you enjoy.

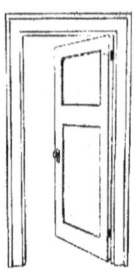

Doorways - Pay attention to portals you encounter. What changes inside you as you pass through them? How do you sense those changes? What do they mean? Can you sense non-physical doorways as well?

Body Focus - As an awareness practice, you can focus your attention into your body—your mind, heart, and general state of being. Allow yourself to go into what you are experiencing. Enjoy it. Then describe the experience for yourself. Be more present and integrated through the awareness of your body experience.

Imagination and Direct Perception - You can use your imagination. Begin to develop inner focus. You can differentiate between imagination and perception. You can fine tune your awareness.

Sense an object - Find an object that interests you. Experience this object with your senses. Notice any changes you experience and describe them.

Drawing - Move into a receptive and passive state of mind. Communicate what you experience without using words.

Chapter 7

Whenever you enjoy drawing or sensing, you might let go and lose yourself a little. Your sense of time may shift. Your mind may relax and become calmer. Your sense of the room around you may soften. Any time your sense of self, the world, or time is altered in some way, you have shifted into a light trance. As in daydreaming, you're still aware, but your orientation to the world around you has shifted. In trance, the conscious mind is not as dominant. With the conscious mind relaxed and passive, the unconscious processes are more free to come to the surface of awareness. Normal unconscious processes like digestion, stress relief, relaxation and healing work more naturally and efficiently when the conscious mind is out of the way. Deeper, unconscious wisdom and intelligence flows more freely through your whole mind/body system. Thus, the trance states you experience can be very beneficial for your total health.

Layers of Consciousness

The trance state of sleep rejuvenates the body. Even lighter states like daydreaming and napping allow our minds to rest and restore. In one study students who napped between tests performed better than non-nappers. 12 The researchers theorized that naps allowed the neural circuits involved in the testing to be refreshed.

I think of the effects of trance on consciousness as being similar to the way we flex and relax muscles. If you hold any muscle in your body tense, it will quite quickly experience fatigue, stress, and signs of disorder. In order to restore it to normal functioning you have to let it relax. The same is true with our consciousness. Since we live in a time of continual demands on our attention, we tend to be always outwardly focused and attentive. If we attend this way for a long time, we experience stress. Thus, shifting into sensation and that more immersed way of attending tends to be stress relieving and relaxing. That is why we daydream. Our unconscious is trying to get us to make a healthy shift in our awareness.

When we enter into the richness of our sensory experience, we come more into balance with the whole mind/body system, including all of our unconscious resources. Both the conscious and unconscious are fundamental aspects of who we are. When we are healthy and attuned to ourselves these parts are balanced and integrated, and one is not more dominant than the other.

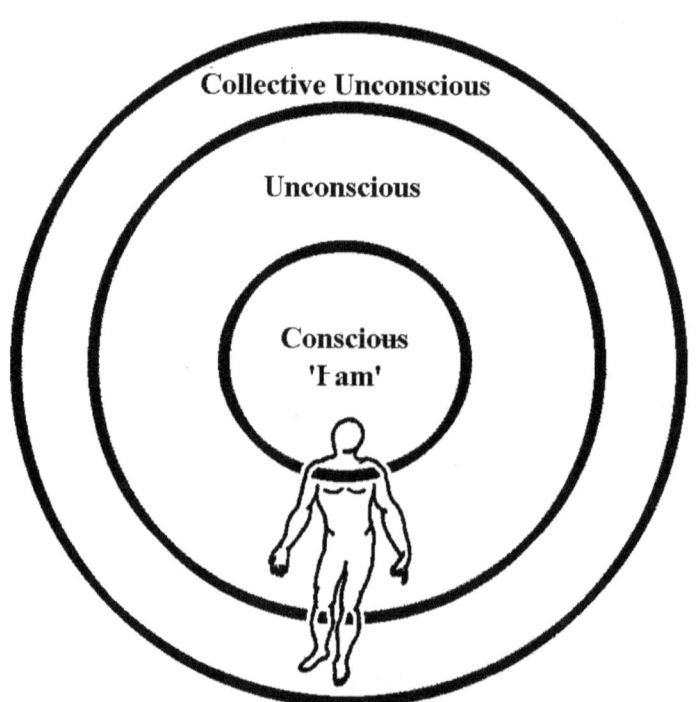

Figure 6 - Layers of Consciousness

Figure 6 offers one way to represent this relationship between conscious, unconscious and higher consciousness parts. Conscious awareness is the center of our ego and self-identity. As the center of our attention, it represents a very small portion of our whole self. The unconscious is the next layer out. It lies at the periphery of conscious awareness. The automatic and expanded functions of the mind, body, and emotions reside in the unconscious. The division between conscious and unconscious is permeable. Many aspects in the unconscious can be accessed consciously. The conscious and unconscious often use different languages. The unconscious communicates in different sensory channels and symbols, which include images.

Farther out on the figure we approach higher consciousness. This is the realm of Carl Jung's collective unconscious, and our awareness of spirit or higher selves. This region is even more removed from conscious awareness. Our individual identity has access to all these layers, but the farther out we go the less our experience is directed by the ego. Our understanding of these more expanded parts is always translated through the subconscious and then by our conscious mental framework and personality.

I put an image of the body over this figure to bring it more into the physical. The head is at the center of consciousness. Typically when we're only in our head, our awareness is limited to what we can hold in conscious awareness. In that state, the division between conscious and unconscious is very distinct. But even when we're in our head we are still connected to the body and the unconscious. It's just that information coming from the unconscious has to be stronger to get through to the conscious mind.

When we extend our awareness beyond what's in our head into our larger body, then the unconscious becomes accessible. The body is a very direct connection to the unconscious. In this figure the body is physical, but it is also symbolic. It is also an extension of our sense of self into emotional and mental spheres. This body also extends into the higher consciousness areas of collective and intuitive reality.

In this figure the areas at the edge of this diagram signify the basis of our conscious experience. We are always immersed in this fundamental ground of being. When we are narrowly focused on our conscious intentions, we are generally not aware of this larger field, except through memory, dream or other unconscious aspects. But there is always a larger percentage of our experiencing body dwelling in the unconscious. That larger, unconscious part of us is also always connected to the ground through the unconscious. Thus the outermost layer in this diagram is also permeable and may even have no limit.

Trance

Shifting into the immersed experience of present moment sensory awareness is a kind of trance. Trance is commonly induced by focusing on some sensory stimulus, such as a sound, breathing, or relaxation. Trance is a natural part of being human. When you make that shift, you may experience it in many different ways, perhaps as a change in body sensation, a shift in the way your thoughts flow, or even an emotional upwelling. Can you remember what it feels like when you start to transition towards sleep? This is another common trance where you begin allowing unconscious processes to come to the surface. When an internal sense or feeling moves to the surface of your awareness, then you've shifted your relationship with your unconscious; you've entered a trance state.

> *Take a moment and remember those last conscious moments before you fell asleep.*
> *Bring to mind your experience of that transition.*
> *Remembering it, can you describe what it's like?*
> *What happens in your mind when you shift into that trance?*

If you haven't paid much attention to these normal altered states of consciousness, it can be difficult to become conscious of them. By remembering the feeling and extending your awareness to that place, you begin to go there. You may even find yourself recollecting dream imagery or other awarenesses you had the last time you were in a similar state.

If you have difficulty recalling the pre-sleep state, then remember the object you sensed. Was there a sense there that you enjoyed or that you allowed yourself to go further into? That was also an en-trance, an opening into a similar trance. Paying attention to your personal trance indicators helps you learn to shift your awareness intentionally.

> *Bring to mind another experience you had that drew you out of yourself.*
> *What were you sensing?*
> *What was happening in your mind, body, or heart?*
> *Remember those sensations and allow some of the feeling to come back.*

You can read about trance now while being connected to your own memory of it. Allow the memories of a trancing experience you had to stay with you as you read.

> *Let your body relax.*
> *Remember the sensation of shifting your awareness while you continue reading.*

Trance and Sensing

Trance isn't an on-or-off experience where you're in it or not. Rather, it has subtle gradations. While you're remembering falling to sleep or into another state, you are shifting a little. When you sense an object, you may also have shifted more. If your mind wanders to something you need to do, or to the sound of someone else moving in your house, your trance may shift again. You are continually shifting your focus, and consequently your trance, anytime your attention is drawn into a different way of perceiving or processing information.

> **Trance is a natural process that allows flexibility of mind and a connection between the conscious and unconscious.**

Trance is a natural process that allows flexibility of mind and a connection between the conscious and unconscious. Even a brief dip into an inner memory, perhaps triggered by a phrase you read here, allows you to connect to a thought or a feeling in a different and meaningful way. If you're focused on reading and you feel a wave of sleepiness, you could stop and nap briefly. Afterwards, your mind and body will feel different. You may find yourself energized. While you're asleep, you may dream about intuitive processes. There is often an intelligence in the way your subconscious moves you away from the focus of your conscious mind.

> *Is your unconscious guiding you now?*
> *Let yourself relax into a light trance of connection to yourself.*
> *You can enjoy the guidance and opening of your whole being.*

> *Keeping this book open as you read, I'd like you to entertain the idea that you can perceive the next visual image or symbol that occurs in the following pages of this book.*
> *You can perceive it intuitively.*
> *You can soften your gaze now, become receptive and focus on your inner vision.*
> *You might want to gently and slowly allow your head to tilt to one side as you shift to perceiving inwards.*
> *Your sensing may temporarily pull you away from the text.*
> *Follow that.*
> *Note any changes or sensations.*
> *Any experience you have may be an intuitive response.*
> *At some point, as you shift into your intuitive sensing, you may want to let your eyes close, if that feels comfortable.*

> *Do it now.*
> *Notice any changes that occur in you.*
> *Then describe what you perceive.*
> *Afterwards, describe all your shifts, changes and flowing of your awareness?*

With each exercise, you are increasing awareness of any changes that occur within you. Tilting your head can be a simple way to invite body or unconscious guidance into your awareness. There may be some other spontaneous body movement that happens spontaneously and guides you. The next time you have an insight or intuitive awareness, notice what's happening in your body. There may be a physical correlation. When you shift into a trance, any one of your senses may be altered in a way you can learn to recognize.

Now you can have feedback for this exercise. Turn to page 207 to see what the target is.

Get your feedback now, then continue reading.

When you look at the graphic, what do you sense?
What is your body response to that image?
Sketch what you perceive to connect with it.

Then notice if there are any connections between what you
*   sensed intuitively and the target image or symbol.*
Circle those connections.

Again, with each exercise you do, remember it's the process and the learning that's important. Just as with this exercise, you can create other easy ways to practice sensing. Be open and explore. Learn from practicing your inner sensing.

You may have been able to perceive a slight shift in your awareness doing the last exercise. En-trances can occur in an infinite number of ways. If you are visually dominant, your awareness of trance may begin with an alteration in your visual field. If you stare at an object and stay focused there, you may start to notice changes in your vision. You might experience blurred or extra-sharp focus, darker or lighter colors, loss of peripheral vision, pulsations in light, intensity and color, multiple vision, or even a general fading of your entire visual field. At some point your eyes will get tired. Then when you close them and let go of your holding focus, you might relax your whole mind and body and go into a deeper trance. This is the beginning of a common induction into self-hypnosis and intuitive visioning.

When these kinds of alterations occur in our vision or in our other senses during normal daytime activities, we often ignore them. Since we're "on task" with our conscious focus, we reestablish our normal vision as quickly as possible. Yet, these subtle shifts may indicate unconscious information wanting to come to consciousness.

When you allow small changes in your sensing or experiencing, these changes may open a flow of intuitive information. Similar visual distortions I have described are utilized by psychics who work with crystal balls. When focused on the ball, the psychic allows her consciousness to shift. Then internal, intuitive images start to arise and are allowed into consciousness. There is nothing special about the ball. It is the changes in the psychic's awareness that opens up her intuition. The ball serves as a visual focus, an entryway into the trance.

As one goes deeper into trance and more into an altered state of awareness, more internal imagery begins to form. David Lewis-Williams, an archaeologist who specializes in prehistoric art, describes how this next step is experienced in trance:

> *People "see" geometric forms, such as dots, zigzags, grids, sets of parallel lines, nested curves, and meandering lines. The forms are brightly colored and flicker, pulsate, enlarge, contract, and blend one with another. With the eyes open, they are projected luminously onto surfaces such as walls and ceilings.* [19]

These visual forms have been discovered in rock art dating back at least thirty thousand years. They are thought to be the record of shamanic altered states. They also occur in drug-induced states of consciousness. These "entoptic" images, or images from within the mind, are transitional phenomena that develop into more complex visual imagery in even deeper trance states. They can evolve into symbolic images and dream-like imagery that can relate specifically to conscious intentions.

If your awareness is centered around another sense, you may experience the same relaxation of perception and alteration. If you focus on the auditory channel, you may experience subtle changes in the background sounds in the space you're in. You may start to hear new sounds, low tones, buzzing or clicking, or words and phrases. Hearing one's name spoken is a common auditory hallucinatory phenomenon. Others report hearing music. As with a visual technique, the auditory stimulus can lead into a flow of increasingly complex "hallucinations". This can occur with any sense.

If your kinesthetic channel is dominant, you might experience the same progression as a range of sensations in the body. Spontaneous muscle twitches may progress into complete physical sensations of movement or other activity.

Becoming adept at utilizing deeper trance states relies on allowing the manifestations of trance as they occur. These manifestations can be difficult in the beginning as any abnormal phenomena may be disconcerting or even overly exciting. Many people focus on phenomena that arise with conscious awareness. For example, have you ever thought you saw something out of the corner of your eye? What happened when you looked at it? Directing your conscious, focused mind on these unconscious signals chases them away. We activate a different state of mind which causes a shift to objective awareness. We terminate the trance state.

As you learn to be more receptive and more comfortable allowing unknown senses and feelings, you can allow subconscious perceptions coming into the periphery of your awareness. You can recognize when something unusual is happening and relax into it, before you try to "look" directly at it and figure out what it is. Any alteration you sense can be the beginning of information coming from your unconscious, whether you call it intuition, insight, or hallucination.

Visual Focus

With all the sensing exercises in this book, you can allow whatever subtle alterations in your consciousness that you deem comfortable. The changes in your consciousness will only happen in a way that feels safe and serves you. With practice, familiarity and comfort, you can invite them to become stronger and clearer.

Here's another exercise to loosen your conscious focus. On the next page you will see a mandala, a geometric symbol used in meditation. You will use that symbol for the exercise.

Read through the exercise first.

Place this book on a table in a way that permits you to relax your body and gaze at the symbol at the same time. Take several comfortable breaths. Relax. As you breathe, gaze at the symbol. You may even focus on one particular spot on the symbol. As you do, repeat a simple phrase to yourself:

As I breathe easier, becoming more relaxed, I focus my gaze on this image.
Thoughts, distractions or other sensations flow easily through my awareness.

Figure 7 - Mandala

Allow the image to fill your awareness. As you rest your gaze there, allow any changes that occur in your vision. Focusing on the image tends to tire the muscles in and around your eyes and overloads the light receptors in your eyes. This is a natural reaction. As that happens, you will notice changes in your perceptions. Allow the muscles around your eyes to soften. Allow your gaze to soften. Your inner attention will begin to shift to other sensations. At some point, your eyes will become tired and want to close. That's natural. When that happens, closing your eyes and letting go will take you into a light, comfortable trance state. You can remind yourself:

As my eyes close, I connect to my unconscious mind.

Then imagine that the image that lingers in your mind becomes a door. You can open that door and pass through it into a deeper connection to your unconscious. Relax and let your unconscious lead. Your experience will unfold in a way that is perfect for you.

When you decide you're finished and you open your eyes, you will be back in a normal state of consciousness. Reflect, describe and draw what you've just experienced.

Important: When you focus on the symbol, it's OK to create some tension in your eyes. But too much strain isn't good. Let your unconscious tell you when to close your eyes. Tell yourself that when you close your eyes it will feel good. Then you can relax and go deeper into yourself. The mandala exercise should be a comfortable experience.

Do the exercise now.
Afterwards, describe everything you experienced.

As you begin to read again, you can let as much of your "altered" state stay with you as you enjoy.

Once you opened the symbolic door in that exercise, your experience could have unfolded in many different ways. What can be experienced is virtually unlimited. There is no right or wrong response, only an exploration of your sensing and your learning how to shift into trance. Your experience may have become dreamlike, may have shifted between different senses, may have been mostly about thoughts and feelings, not made sense, or not really been much of anything. The meaning of your experience may not be rational, but it still has value.

Repeat this exercise if you want. Each time you open the door be receptive to whatever enters your awareness. As you become more familiar with the process, it will become easier; you will allow yourself to shift into unconscious guidance.

If you hold an intention in your mind as you do the exercise, then when you go through the door, your experience will correlate to any intention you have. You can also use this visual door as a way to move towards an intuitive target. Just state your intent first. Then let go and allow whatever comes through your unconscious. If you go into trance without a conscious intent, you will be led by deeper intentions; you will be viewing yourself or some deeper part of you. You can use this exercise any time you wish to explore yourself.

What does your experience from this exercise tell you about yourself?

The more you attend to your own shifting, the more you build a connection to your unconscious. Initially, these changes may have no meaning for you. But with time, you will start to identify personal markers of the trance state that carry meaning.

Several different phenomena occur to me when I shift into a trance state. Sometimes I get a sense that I am in the middle of a large space or field. This opening isn't related to my physical surroundings. Sometimes the feeling of the skin on my upper body changes. It's as if I am touching something physical that energizes me. I often feel a prickling sensation on the backs of my hands and arms. The skin and muscles of my face relax and get heavier. Also, there may be a warm energy in my chest, at the heart level. Sometimes there is a slightly acidic taste in my mouth and I salivate.

These perceptions do not happen all at once. Sometimes I notice only one of these markers. Other times I'm not aware of any of them. If I'm focused on one sense, as in the above exercise, that may be the only channel I'm aware of. When I want to enter into trance, bringing these familiar sensations up, starts me moving in that direction. As I remember the feeling of trance, a shift in my consciousness is initiated. Other times, the trance state comes first. I may suddenly realize I am already in trance and the shift was entirely outside my conscious awareness.

> *When you sense a change within you, allow it.*
> *You can make it conscious and describe it.*

If you're not used to idling your conscious mind as these exercises encourage, or if you have some negative preconceptions about words like "trance" and "hypnosis," your experience of trance may be uncomfortable. Your body might twitch, or your eyes might shift, or thoughts might distract you. Whatever you experience, even if it is uncomfortable, you can still stay present. It is your process. Distracting thoughts may be your conscious mind trying to maintain control.

If your experience becomes too uncomfortable, remember you can change it. You can take care of yourself. You may sense a need to change something, in your body, mind, spirit or heart. You may need to recognize a fear or a limiting belief, and let it go. Regardless what you experience, you can respond with your whole being. If your desire is to expand your awareness, then give yourself time. Be patient. With each exercise, you are building bridges to larger parts of your self.

If you enjoy letting go of your conscious mind, that simple exercise may have been energizing and refreshing. Trance states allow you to access creativity, insight and intuition. In trance, you can open a meaningful connection to yourself.

> *So there is a greater intelligence in human beings than can be contained in the human mind. The mind is only a tiny aspect of this greater intelligence, which is the same intelligence that created the galaxies and the world of nature.*
>
> — Eckhart Tolle
> 13

Chapter 8

Further Opening to the Unconscious

Light trances, such as day dreaming, can be used intentionally to free up the intuitive process. Thomas Edison used altered states to stimulate his creativity. When he reached a creative impasse, he used a very simple method of trance induction. He would sit in his chair and rest his hands on his legs. In one hand he'd hold some marbles. Then he would let himself drift towards sleep. As his body relaxed, his conscious mind would let go, he would start to fall asleep. As he transitioned into sleep, his hands would relax and the marbles would fall to the floor. The sound of the marbles hitting the floor would wake him.

The short span of time between relaxing and the sound waking him allowed only a brief shift in consciousness; he would never fall into deep sleep. Still, that brief time recharged his energies. He would sometimes awaken with an insight about the task he was working on.

The German chemist August Kekule's discovery of the benzene molecule ring is a similar example. Kekule had struggled to comprehend the structure of the compound. When he stopped to rest, he fell asleep and had a "dream" where he saw the atoms dancing around before his eyes in long rows that looked like snakes. As he continued dreaming, he noticed that one of the snakes had its own tail in its mouth. As he perceived this image he woke up. It was then he realized the image represented the structure of the molecule. [22]

His perception of the circular shape of the snake-like structure turned out to be an accurate intuition of the shape of the molecule. Kekule had lapsed into a hypnagogic trance/dream state that occurs at the threshold between waking and sleeping. In this state there is some sense of waking consciousness and at the same time there is dreamlike imagery from the subconscious. He had all the knowledge of the structures he was working with in his unconscious, but until then he hadn't been able to make the conscious connection.

There are many different languages or channels for the flow of information from the unconscious. Lois Isenman [19] suggests that our feelings may be signals from the unconscious that lead us to the information we seek. This emotional intelligence can move much faster than thought. She says our feelings are part of a larger, unconscious, yet logical process similar to our conscious logic. The primary difference between conscious and unconscious processing is that the unconscious seems to be much faster and able to contain much more information.

Some researchers go so far as to say that most processing is unconscious. John Bargh [11], a psychological researcher, calls our unconscious mental processes "mental butlers" referring to how they look out for us and know our intentions often before we're consciously aware of them. For example, have you ever had the experience of driving along in a trance or a daydream and then suddenly becoming focused and alert just before you consciously see a deer? That experience may have been your own mental butler looking out for you!

Researchers like Bargh find that the idea of conscious control is highly overrated and suggest it occurs much less that we imagine. Our unconscious processes serve us and direct our behavior far beyond the scope of what we are consciously aware. Any practice you do to connect with your unconscious can put you directly in contact with resources and ways of knowing that can seem extraordinary.

The further we go from our normal conscious, ego orientation, the less we are limited by our beliefs and limitations. When we are in a profoundly altered state, we can experience ourselves as boundless with unlimited potential. It is often in extreme altered states that deeply impactful intuitions occur. You might experience a telepathic connection with distant loved ones, visions of significant future events, or even personal insights that might trigger a spontaneous remission of a disease.

The vision quest within some Native American traditions is one example of a ritual that intentionally creates an altered state and a peak experience. Through dehydration, exposure to the elements, fasting, and strong intention, an individual is shaken out of his normal perception of reality. When he "breaks through" he may experience a connection with a spirit or spirit guides, a sense of his life's purpose, a spontaneous healing, or the realization of specific information he was seeking. When the seeker returns to normal consciousness, their elders help them remember and integrate their experiences so they can bring their insights and experiences back to the rest of their community.

> *The further we go from our normal conscious, ego orientation, the less we are limited by our beliefs and limitations.*

This kind of ritual use of altered states serves a very important social function and its value is recognized. In many so-called primitive cultures altered states are still highly valued. To recognize the value of altered states, modern people need to begin paying attention to them.

Though these extreme altered states are attractive and mysterious, less profound states also have positive effects. After experiencing a sensual massage or viewing a relaxing sunset, we may feel a new sense of vitality. With each transition we recognize as meaningful, we build these altered states into our lives. Much like a Hatha Yoga practice with its physical postures, we can gain the ability to move in and out of discrete altered states. We can consciously choose the best state of consciousness for a certain part of our life. Even peak, life-changing experiences may manifest spontaneously when we've learned to trust our connection to larger forces and when we've created a ritual space to experience them. Whatever the experience, with each trance we can integrate what we've learned into normal consciousness.

Each exercise in this book is about this subtle expanding and stretching of your state of mind. With familiarity, you can go deeper. Each altered state becomes part of the flow of your becoming, returning you to "now," this moment, this breath. Your guide to what is right for you in this moment is inside you. When you create a relationship with your unconscious, you allow greater guidance from your soul.

> *Once again, remember the feeling of a high, or profound experience you have had.*
> *There is a wisdom in that kind of letting go.*
>
> *You can allow your own intelligence to guide you in a way that's just right.*
> *Even in your dreams tonight you may continue to expand on your insights from these exercises.*

While you are reading this book, do you find yourself spacing out or drifting off somewhere? Embrace that shift as a manifestation of your own intelligence. Go with it. Stop reading and trust yourself. A shift to a different state can be just as brief as an embrace with a loved one. A deep breath, connected to the sense of letting go, can be very meaningful.

> *Take a slow, relaxed breath.*
>
> *Enjoy yourself.*

Each time you come back to your breath, you shift your awareness and build the consciousness flexibility I've been talking about. You return to the larger presence of your being. Each time you check in with yourself, there may be a message waiting for you, an instant message waiting in your "in" box. Each time you allow this guidance, your intuition becomes a more accessible part of your being. Then you can flow back to this focus again and another kind of trance learning.

Breathing Focus

Becoming aware of the breath is a powerful way to come back into the present. You can consciously speed up your breath or slow it down. Then, when your attention is elsewhere, your unconscious regulates your breathing. Your breath is a natural bridge between the conscious and unconscious.

The next exercise is a form of meditation that uses breath. Again, read through this exercise first.

> *Become aware of the breath coming in and out of your body.*
> *Feel the sensation of the breath in your body, expanding and contracting.*
> *You may hear your breath as well as feel it as a bodily sensation.*
> *Allow the breath to flow in and out naturally, as if it were guiding you.*
> *Let it find its own rhythm, not too fast or too slow.*
> *Enjoy the felt sense of your breath.*
>
> *You can let your eyes be open or closed, whichever is comfortable to you.*
>
> *Then, at some point, when you get to the end of an exhalation, begin counting softly inside your mind: "One."*
> *Repeat the number softly in your mind as you breathe through the inhalation and the next exhalation. "One, one, one..."*
> *Say the number softly, as many times as is comfortable for you through that complete breath. You can say it once, or repeat it several times.*
> *Let this counting fall into a comfortable rhythm.*
> *At the end of that exhalation, say the next number in your mind, "Two, two, two," increase the number each time you get to the end of a breath.*

As you count, continue to be aware of the sensation of breathing.
You will enter into a more relaxed, yet focused, meditative state.
Let yourself sink into it.
Whenever you notice that your awareness of your breath has wandered away from your counting - then start over again at "One."
Return to the breath and let it guide you.
As you practice you will find that it's OK when your mind wanders. You will be able to stay with the numbers as you stay in that focused, receptive state for longer periods.
As other sensations, thoughts or feelings pass through you, stay with the breath and the numbers.

Do the entire breathing exercise now.
Take your time.

When you sense you've done enough, take a moment and describe your experience.

How did this exercise make you feel?
Was it comfortable or uncomfortable?
Was it difficult to focus your awareness?
Where did your mind go when it wandered?
Did that wandering carry any meaning for you?

Focusing on the breath allows a gradual stilling of your mind, opening a deeper connection to yourself. With practice, you can allow whatever manifests in your consciousness without having to respond. As your breathing continues, the unconscious will lead you to other places. You can have a very profound exercise and even the basis of a meditative practice. If you enjoyed this exercise, do it often. Adapt it to suit you better.

Intuitive Perception

You already have the tools you need to be intuitive. I have

chosen a target for you to perceive intuitively. I'm not going to tell you what it is beforehand. Not knowing encourages you to use your non-physical senses. The target could be anything in the world, anything imaginable. The target is the focal point for your intuitive perception for this exercise. I'll tell you what it is after you're done so you'll be able to get feedback.

Note: When you are finished with this exercise, you will need to access the internet to get feedback for this target. If you don't have internet access, you can still do this exercise and several others further in the book. However, you may want to pause here and look at Appendix A on page 287 to see how to create some intuitive targets for yourself. This is easy to do and can be a fun part of learning intuition. If you have internet access, then continue reading.

Read through this entire exercise first, and then enjoy it on your own. To begin, I'd like you to take a few more relaxing breaths. Remember feeling the sun on your body again, or remember any other comfortable memory.

Take your time.
Relax, and enjoy yourself.
Enjoy the senses you imagine.
There's no need to hurry.
Let your comfort lead you.
Enjoy your comfortable memory until you feel a shift into greater calmness and receptivity.

When your mind is a little quieter, give yourself permission to perceive the "target." Say to yourself:

"It's OK to perceive with my intuition."
Then you can state an intention;
"I want to perceive the target now."

Then let go of that intent and be open to what is happening within you. You don't have to do anything. Whatever you experience will be a response to your intuitive intent. It may be a specific sensation, a different emotion, or a new thought. Whatever you experience will relate in some way to your intention to perceive the target. Allow whatever comes and be patient. Give yourself a few moments for your mind to relax. Something will appear in your consciousness. Perhaps it is already forming.

Then write, draw and describe everything you sense or experience. Remember, nothing is trivial. Even if you think you're just experiencing your thoughts and worries, describe them anyhow. It's all part of the flow of your awareness and it's all a learning process. Stay with describing your experience until you feel you've gone far enough.

You can go through the process now....

Then continue reading when you're done describing.

Did you write down or draw everything during this experience? Communication is important. If you don't express your perceptions through drawing, writing, or speaking, it might not be as meaningful to you later. Also, expressing allows you to release what you're experiencing, bringing you back to the here and now. This process is the same as the body focus when you attend to your physical body and your external senses through the body focus. Attention and description of what is happening allows it to release. If there's any response you'd like to make or need to make, you can do so now. You will be more present in the now with yourself as a result.

Listening inwards again, is there anything you need?
Does your body need movement, water, or food?

You can respond to what is alive in you.
It's important to validate the needs of your body.

Feedback

Now you can get the feedback to your first intuition experiment. An image of this target is located on the website for this book. You can find it at www.AJoyfulIntuition.com/Target1.jpg. (If you have created your own target for this exercise, you can open it now.)

Look at your target picture before reading any further.

Now, after initially viewing your feedback picture, I want you to take some time with it and give it your attention. Your target is actually what is shown in the picture, not just the image itself. It may include all your senses, emotions, or other more complex information. Your dominant feedback is visual, but you can extrapolate in your mind what your other senses would experience at the target.

Important: Let each of your senses tune into the target, as if you were there. Describe what you perceive or imagine you would perceive if you were there. Write down these descriptions. Your mind probably has already labeled it and defined it, but by perceiving and describing you connect with the target outside of your label of it. You move out of critical and judgmental thinking into a more receptive frame of mind.

Sense and describe that target now.
Feel free to sketch parts of it that grab your attention.
Describe what you would perceive with all of your senses.

Now after you've described the actual target, go back and look at what you wrote intuitively, before you opened the envelope. See if there are any sensations, colors or shapes that feel connected to the target. You are just going on what your perception is. Is there a connection with one thing you wrote or another? Circle anything you described that feels connected. Don't be quick to discount descriptions that are not obvious connections. If it feels like there's a connection, circle it. Whatever you sensed and described intuitively is important, regardless of whether it makes sense or not.

Notice and circle any of your intuitive perceptions that feel connected to the target.

Doing this exercise with attention is what's most important. If what you wrote doesn't make sense, that's OK. Perhaps you didn't circle anything. There may be a deeper meaning in it, or not. When you do intuitive exercises, you will sometimes get hits or connections, and sometimes not. It's all part of learning how your consciousness works! Welcome it all. You can ask yourself if there is a meaning to something you described that is symbolic or metaphorical.

You may also recognize that some of your descriptions came wholly from your conscious mind, perhaps remembering a color or another sense you recently experienced. Sometimes guessing or grabbing for knowns may be easier than the awkwardness of waiting for something unknown to arrive. If you did that in this last exercise, be aware of the feelings and thoughts you were experiencing. Being conscious of them and describing them will help you relax into the unknowing of intuitive perception. Even now after getting feedback, you are still learning things about yourself and how your awareness moves.

All the exercises in this book will give you feedback. With quick feedback, you will be able to consciously connect your intuitive experience to something tangible, an important part of learning intuition. This way you will start to learn the subtle difference between perception and imagination.

Having said that, there is still tremendous value in using your intuition even when you don't get feedback. That's when intuitive perceptions are the most profound—when you act with knowing and trust yourself. Feedback helps you trust yourself. Yet, even with all the feedback you get, it's your inner experience that you're learning to trust. In the end, only you will know what value or meaning your perceptions have. You start by validating what you are experiencing now, even if you label it incorrect in your mind.

Take a moment now for more reflection.

Having done this intuitive exercise, how do you feel?
Start with what you are experiencing now - thoughts, feelings, senses...
Go through the body focus again and describe what you are

sensing.
(Refer to the diagram on page 37 to remember all the channels of perception.)
As you go through each channel, you may notice differences from the last time you checked in.
Be sure to describe those differences.

Has something in your body changed? A feeling or a state of mind?
If you have an inner sense or an outer one, meaningful or not, describe it and make it conscious.
You can even describe feelings that are in you that you don't understand.
It's OK to not know and still describe.
As you become more aware of the flow of your awareness, you will become more receptive, responsive, and sensitive to changes that occur in you.

Chapter 9

Body and Ideomotor Signals

As you focus on your breath, you calm your mind. A calm mind allows you to perceive what is alive and active in your larger body. Your body is the primary channel through which the unconscious manifests in your awareness. It's easy to observe your body as external to your self, as an object, but it's also intimately connected with your consciousness. Every thought and feeling in your awareness is mirrored in some way in the body, and vice versa. Twitches, itches, heat flashes, and other spontaneous body movements are messages from the unconscious.

An unconscious or involuntary body response that comes from a thought, feeling or an idea, rather than from an external stimulus, is called an ideomotor response. Ideomotor literally means the idea-movement. An example of an ideomotor response might be a chill or tension in your stomach when you think of something fearful. When you think of a sunset, your ideomotor response will probably generate different bodily sensations.

How does your unconscious respond to a sunset?

Say an itch develops during your breathing exercise. The itch may be caused by something on your skin or it might not relate to anything tangible or recognizable. The itch may be an ideomotor response connected to something in your unconscious. Though these kinds of physical movements may make no logical sense, if they are allowed into consciousness, they can become meaningful. When you are listening to a lecture, for instance, you may nod when you agree with the ideas. You may not be conscious of either the nodding or your agreement, but your unconscious is still communicating. You may even consciously agree with something while your unconscious disagrees.

Do you know what happens in your body when you know something is wrong?

Perhaps your stomach tightens up or you get a chill. This is your ideomotor response. As you become more in touch with how your unconscious communicates, you can pay attention to its signals even when they contradict what you think consciously.

Sensing these ideomotor signals in the body is the basis of kinesiology. In kinesiology, muscle responses are interpreted in simple terms of right and wrong, or "yes" and "no." The response you feel in your stomach also occurs in muscles throughout the body. You can notice the difference in any muscles you pay attention to, fingers or arms being the most common. Typically with a "yes" response a muscle is stronger, a "no" response is weaker. The response is generally stronger when there is more importance to the "yes" or "no." Since you can control your muscles consciously, you get more accurate muscle responses when your conscious mind is relaxed and detached.

Dowsing is a method that uses these same subtle ideomotor responses. Dowsing uses an external tool to amplify the unconscious responses in the body. A pendulum or a dowsing rod is perhaps the most common dowsing instrument. It only takes micro-muscular movements in the hand or arm to generate a visible response in the

> **Dowsing uses an external tool to amplify the unconscious responses in the body.**

movement of these instruments. The force that moves the pendulum comes from the unconscious, through the body. The unconscious may have information gathered through normal sensory means or it may be operating with intuitive information. I personally believe there are no other outside forces, magnetic fields or subtle energies that are physically causing the pendulum to move. That may not be true for you though if your intention is to perceive these external forces.

Inviting an ideomotor response is essentially giving some control of your mind and body over to your unconscious. An essential distrust of the unconscious is pervasive in our modern society. Any uncontrolled or spontaneous behavior that isn't clearly "sensible" is frowned upon. From an early age we are conditioned to be still, quiet, and in control. We are punished for lack of control and thus learn to fear it when it happens. When children fidget in their seats in school, their movements are coming from their unconscious, trying to bring some comfort, balance, or even movement into their bodies. By stilling them, we are essentially teaching them it's more important to conform than to honor their own intelligence.

If you've never consciously recognized the unconscious aspects of your being, your ideomotor response might be surprising, even threatening. You might even think the forces you feel in your body are caused by a malevolent force or entity. If so, it would be helpful to journal a little bit about your beliefs. Remember the wisdom you are accessing within you can be tremendously wise. You can learn to trust yourself again.

This is one reason I encourage you to move when you feel the need, even if it doesn't make sense. (This may even mean putting down this book, if that's what feels right to you!) When you attend to what you are sensing for yourself, you validate your own wisdom. Your action may be something that helps you bring your body back into health and balance. Sitting and reading for hours at a time is not natural; movement is. If you've restricted these spontaneous ideomotor movements your whole life, then a healthy "relaxing" response may manifest more as movement, release, and physical letting go. These unconditioned movements may feel awkward, but they do have value. The larger part of your being is always seeking your best health and well-being.

Pendulum

Using a dowsing tool can be very helpful for getting in touch with your own ideomotor process. Remember, there is no power inherent in the pendulum itself. It is in you. Here's a nice analogy about dowsing from Jeffrey Mishlove's book, <u>Psi Development Systems</u>:

> We may liken the radionics (dowsing) instrument to a pencil. If you were asked to multiply 123 times 178 in your head, the task might well seem impossible. However, if you had a pencil and paper, it would be no problem to go through the step by step multiplication procedure. Even using the pencil, nobody would think that it was not you who did the arithmetic. Nobody would suggest that there was a magic "pencil power" which was able to solve mathematical problems. In fact, if you tried you could probably train yourself to do mathematics without the use of a pencil at all. [25]

Similarly, the pendulum makes accessing the unconscious easier but it isn't the source of the movements or the information provided. Once you develop a relationship with your unconscious, you may be able to dispense with the dowsing tool altogether. Accomplished dowsers know the pendulum or forked stick isn't always necessary. In a crunch they will simply tell you the answer. Yet they still use the tool since its familiarity puts them into a comfortable and relaxed ritual space.

Here is an easy progression to start your exploration of a pendulum. Try each suggestion and see what happens. Your unconscious will respond in just the right way for you.

Remember to take notes.
What are you experiencing now?

First, find a pendulum. You can use any small weight on a piece of string, cord or chain. The weight can be just about anything you can tie to a string, though something symmetrical is usually preferred, so it doesn't wobble erratically. You want something that has weight, but that is not so heavy that your arm gets tired. A necklace with a weighted pendant will work. You can also tie a washer onto a piece of string. One of the simplest pendulums is a paper clip attached to a piece of thread, though the paper clip is a little on the light side.

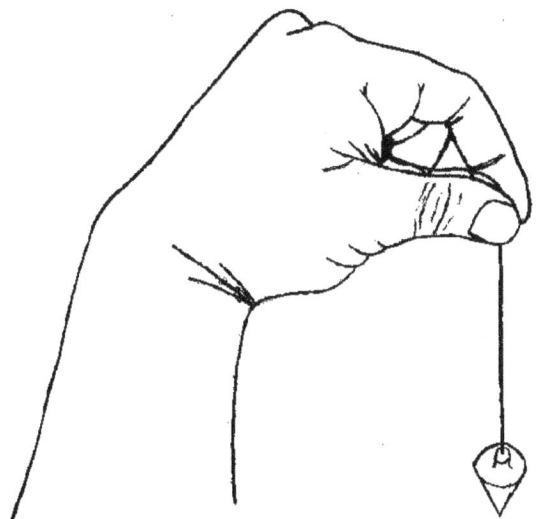

Figure 8 - Holding a Pendulum

Hold your pendulum with the string between the thumb and first finger, as illustrated in Figure 8. Rest your elbow on a table or against your body so your arm will not tire. For an average sized pendulum allow between 3 and 6 inches of string between your fingers and the weight. Wrap any extra string around the other fingers. This position allows free movement of the pendulum. Experiment with the movement. Swing it around with your hand. If it's too fast and erratic, you can lengthen the string. If it responds too slowly, shorten it. With practice, you'll find a length that feels comfortable to you.

Pendulum use starts with the weight moving in a neutral position, one that doesn't have any meaning. For now, a diagonal movement will be neutral, though it doesn't matter which movement is chosen. See figure 9 page 114. The perspective of this figure is as if you were looking down on your pendulum from above.

Swing the pendulum in the direction of one of the diagonals and rest your mind on this movement so that it keeps swinging this way. Say to yourself either aloud or in your mind, "Neutral position."

Do this now.
Enjoy this movement for a minute or so.

As you watch the movement of the pendulum, your breathing can relax and your awareness may shift into a light trance. This simple movement can be relaxing and meditative. You can allow your mind to begin shifting out of conscious dominance into a more receptive frame of mind.

Remember that receptive feeling?
Let it guide you.

It takes a very slight effort to keep the pendulum oscillating in this neutral position. There are muscles involved, but with practice, you can turn those muscles over to your unconscious.

Your awareness can shift to a more passive mode.
You might imagine you are watching a pendulum being held in someone else's hand.
How does that feel?

If it slows down altogether and stops, then give it more energy. You do want enough movement to be easily recognizable. From this position you can begin exploring "yes" and "no" responses. So read the following paragraphs, and then continue with the exercise.

Close your eyes while holding the pendulum and allowing it to swing.

Bring to mind a place where you feel comfortable, relaxed and safe.

Allow the feeling of that safe, comfortable place to return to your awareness.

Remember what you sensed when you were there.
Remember the smells...
the sounds...
the tastes...
colors...
and even the sensations on your skin...

Let all those positive feelings come back into your body. Enjoy them.

When you have a strong physical sense of this comfortable place, then say to yourself, "Yes." This is a place where your whole being says, "Yes." Your conscious and unconscious agree. Say and feel, "Yes," throughout your whole body and mind. Now, gently open your eyes while keeping the feeling of "Yes" in your body. In fact, as you open your eyes, imagine the feeling of "Yes" and the word "Yes" are more important than what you see with your eyes.

Then with a soft gaze, watch the pendulum and allow your feelings to be your primary focus. Be aware how it's moving. Enjoy the movement. The way the pendulum is moving is connected to your feeling of "Yes." As you watch it, say, "Yes" in your mind. Since every muscle in your body resonates with the yes place you imagine, the way it is moving is your "Yes" response right now.

Do it now.
Get in touch with your "Yes" place.
Feel it throughout your body.
Observe the pendulum and say "Yes."

Then take a moment and describe what that felt like so far.
Also describe the movement of the pendulum.
You can let your pendulum rest as you do this.

There are basically five ways your pendulum will respond:

1 - It will be oscillating like a clock pendulum, from side to side.
2 - It will be oscillating like a swing, forward and back.
3 - It will be oscillating on one of the diagonals.
4 - It will be rotating in a clockwise circular movement.
5 - It will be rotating in a counter-clockwise circular movement.
6 - It will stop moving.

Also, it may be moving in some combination of these movements.

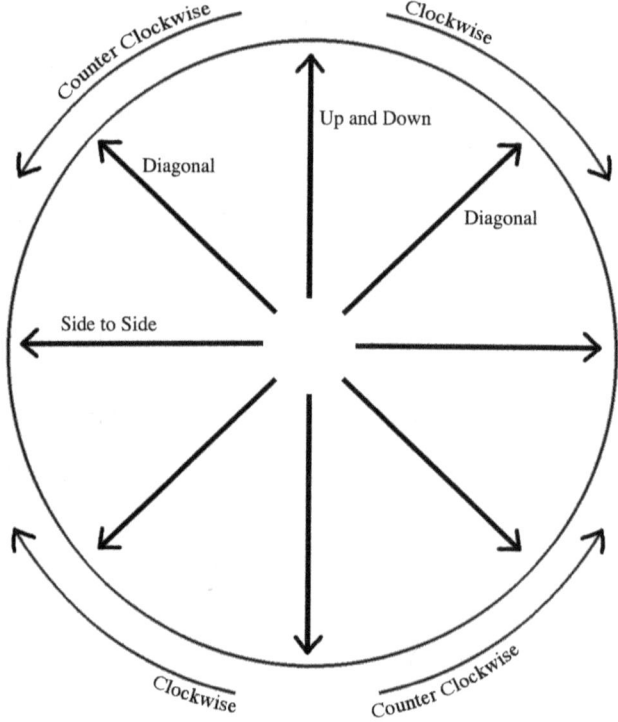

Figure 9 - Pendulum Movements

However your pendulum is moving, enjoy it. As you watch it, notice how it focuses your conscious mind. Continue thinking,

"Yes" in your mind every once in a while. Continue remembering the feeling of your "Yes" place. You may feel your conscious mind partially controlling these movements. When you're learning to access your unconscious, the conscious mind may be involved. If you enjoy its movement and allow it move through you, it will gradually become a more natural, automatic process.

If your pendulum is still or moving very slightly, then it might be helpful to make a stronger connection to your positive feelings. It actually takes effort to be completely still, so you may actually be holding yourself back. Let yourself breathe. Let the sense of your "Yes" place flow through you. The "Yes" feeling can move in your body as you become alive with it. Your hand or arm may move. That's fine. Allow it. Don't resist your feelings. In order to feel good and comfortable you have to let go a little. Letting go isn't always about being still. Sometimes it's an active process.

Once you recognize a "Yes" movement in your pendulum allow it to go back to neutral. Just change the movement consciously by moving your hand until it's swinging in the diagonal position again. If your "Yes" feeling was a diagonal, then pick a different movement for your neutral position, perhaps the other diagonal. Make the pendulum swing in that neutral position and say, "Neutral" in your mind.

Once you're back in neutral, then close your eyes. Remember a place or a situation that you don't like. Remember the experience with all your senses. Again, take your time to really feel it. When you feel it strongly in your body, say to yourself, "No. This is my No feeling." Repeat the word in your mind and body as you feel the "No" feeling. Then again, gradually open your eyes, while holding the feeling in your mind and body and passively observe the pendulum. Passively watch the feeling that has manifested in your pendulum. Enjoy the clear communication of your unconscious saying, "No," and repeat that "No" to yourself.

If you want a stronger response, say and feel "No" louder inside yourself. Remember, sometimes it's important to say "No" to protect yourself, or to stand your ground. It might be helpful to remember a time when you said "No" in a personally empowered way. You can also ask yourself a question where you know the answer is "No." "Do I live in Bangkok?" (Assuming you don't...) Then say "No" to yourself with confidence.

Do it now.
Get in touch with your "No" place.
Feel it throughout your body.
Observe the pendulum and say "No."

Afterwards, take a moment and be aware your responses to using a pendulum.

What are you experiencing now?
Write down your observations.

If you had difficulty getting a response with your pendulum, it may help to tell yourself, "It's OK to relax and let go just to see what happens." If you feel your conscious mind is partially controlling the pendulum, that's OK. You can initiate the process consciously and learn how it feels. With practice, you can have a more reliable connection to your unconscious.

Also, for many people the "No" response is very small or sometimes nonexistant. Many of us haven't learned how to say, "No" from a place of personal strength. If you have a small "No" response, tell yourself, "It's OK to say no!" Saying "No" is a healthy way to take care of yourself. Another reason you may have a still response to "No," is because that's how you say "No." You may get still or freeze. If this happens to you, then encourage yourself to fully express your "No." Again, remind yourself it is important to say "No". No movement may be an accurate "No" response from your pendulum.

Basic Questions

Once you have established basic "Yes" and "No" responses with your pendulum, you can ask yourself a question and see how your unconscious responds. Set your pendulum swinging in the neutral position. Then ask a "Yes" or "No" question to which you will get some feedback in the near future. For example, you could ask, "Do I have mail today?" or "Is (a friend) home now?" Then let go of the question, relax, stay passive, and observe any changes that manifest in your pendulum. Take your time. Watch and enjoy the movement. Be curious, relaxed and open. When you see it begin to change, give it time, and watch the movement again as if it were someone else's hand holding it. When you've received an answer, write it down. Then go get your feedback. Call that person or check your mail. Feedback is important.

Is there a question you want to ask?
Do it now.

When you're done, get feedback.
Describe your experience.

Once you have feedback, it can help to hold your pendulum again, state your question, and say the correct answer in your mind. Allow and encourage your pendulum to swing to the correct answer. You are conditioning your ideomotor response.

Repeat your question with your pendulum.
Help it to "answer" the question with the correct answer.

If you use the pendulum regularly, you will become much more aware of the subtle ideomotor signaling that is always occurring in your body. Every thought or feeling you experience has a physical counterpart. If you think of a close friend, your body will respond one way. If you think of someone that you don't like, the response will be different. The difference may be subtle, but you can learn to discern the difference. When a question arises and you don't have your pendulum, you can observe and trust how your body responds.

> **Every thought or feeling you experience has a physical counterpart.**

Unconscious signaling isn't limited to muscular changes. The quality of your senses may also change. Your vision may become subtly sharper when you're feeling "Yes" or your palms may feel sweatier when you're feeling "No." Any alteration in your awareness can be recognized as useful information.

Sticky Fingers

Here's a useful variation for your pendulum. Repeat the pendulum exercise, but instead of holding a pendulum, use your thumb and forefinger. Lightly touch the tips of these fingers together, and then slightly move them against each other so you can continue to feel that light touch. Go into your "Yes" and "No" places as you did with the pendulum. Notice how the stickiness between your fingers changes depending on if you're feeling "Yes" or "No." The amount of friction as an ideomotor signal is just as accurate as the pendulum. If you pay attention, you will probably find other ideomotor signals that are already serving you. A spontaneous sense of warmth in your heart may be the "Yes" response to the memory of a close friend or something else important.

Using Your Ideomotor Response.

Once you learn the basics of the pendulum and other ideomotor responses in your body, you can use them consciously whenever you have a question to ask. If you're concerned about which foods will be healthy to your body, you can ask your unconscious first. Make sure to phrase your questions clearly. For example, you might ask yourself, "Is this food healthy for me now?" Another way of phrasing the question might be, "Will my body feel good after eating this food?" Then use your pendulum and see what response you get. With this kind of questioning, you will want to relax and quiet your conscious mind first. You may consciously want to eat the food in question, so it takes practice to relax and let whatever answer comes.

Whatever the results are, you can go ahead and decide to eat the food or not, depending on whatever other means of choosing you have. If you do eat it though, pay attention to how you feel afterwards. That way you will get feedback. If you practice, you will learn to trust your own responses more.

Pause...

You can remember and revisit things you enjoy.

Trance - Focus your awareness and change your orientation to reality. Enjoy the benefits of altering your awareness. You can create flexibility in your awareness.

Visual Focus - Focus your gaze on an object or a mandala. Allow the visual field to begin to shift as the receptors in the eyes tire. Then close the eyes and allow your awareness to go inwards following an intuitive intention.

Intuition - You can intend to perceive something, such as an event or an object. Allow your subtle inner perceptions into your awareness. Then, get feedback.

Breathing - Use your breath to calm your mind and body, balance your awareness and connect with the unconscious.

Ideomotor - Use a pendulum to ask yourself questions. Use a passive, receptive frame of mind to communicate with your unconscious.

Chapter 10

Envision an Object

Now you can activate your senses with intention. The next exercise is an extension of the exercise you did earlier, describing an object, except now you can use your inner visioning. For this exercise you will need another interesting object not currently with you, one that you will be able to physically touch when you are done with the exercise. Read through the entire exercise before starting.

> *Remember another interesting object not with you now.*
> *As you bring it into your awareness, explore your sense of it as if it were physically with you.*

> *See the color of it.*
> *Move it in your mind and notice how it feels.*
> *How does the image change when you move it?*
> *Feel the texture of it in your hands or against different parts of your body.*
> *Does it feel different as you handle it?*
> *Does it make a sound when you touch it or move it?*
> *How does it taste?*

Let your inner sensing lead you.
Notice other body responses you have.
Be aware of any subtle changes you experience.

When your inner perceptions become clearer, then shift to description.
Describe you experience as accurately as you can.
Be detailed.
Work your way through all of your senses and feelings.
If you don't have a word to describe a sense or a feeling you're experiencing, then sit with it a bit longer.
Not having words may mean you haven't experienced this particular perception before. Enjoy the newness of this perception. Words may come that don't make sense.

Draw the basic shapes of the object.
Put down a line, an angle, a circle, a pattern of color, or a texture.
Your drawing doesn't have to "look" correct; just draw what you sense.
What you draw may be a descriptive response for a sense that isn't visual.

If more words come while you're drawing, write them down too.

As you're sensing, you may have other perceptions or thoughts that seem unrelated. You may perceive something that you know isn't even related to the object. Whatever comes to you now, as part of your process, describe it.
You can describe your way through your whole experience, including the end of the experience when you come back to reading.
Even when you turn your intent away from your object you can be present.

Do it now.

Is your awareness different now?
Are you feeling different?

Describing in this imaginal way can be very helpful to open up your intuitive perception. You may have noticed how, as you relaxed into it, you could imagine and sense clearly. Your skill will get clearer with practice.

As soon as you get a chance, go and sense your object with your physical senses. As with all the intuitive exercises, connecting your inner experience to tangible feedback is important. When you get your feedback, sense it, describe it and sketch its shape, just as you did above. Then look back again at what you described from your inner visioning. Notice the differences between what you perceived with your inner visioning and your physical perceptions. You can learn from these differences. In some ways, your inner visioning may be clearer and may perceive things you wouldn't attend to with your physical senses. You may also notice with both ways of sensing how your mind comes in and affects what you perceive.

Are there any surprising contrasts between your inner and
  outer senses?

Remember, this type of perception isn't about getting it "right". You are building a connection with your inner sensory experience. You are learning how to be present and describe your experience. You are learning how to be clear in your intention and, at the same time, allow what is happening.

Inner visioning is an effective tool for heightening your internal perceptions. Intuitive sensing is more subtle than physical sensing. Your perceptions are drowned out by the intensity of your immediate physical senses. Over time, with practice, your ability to perceive subtle, intuitive messages will increase. Inner visioning makes your outer senses sharper and your mind clearer. You can bring to mind what you want to do, perceive or explore and you can then get clearer information.

Intention

Our intentions guide the flow of information coming into our awareness. For instance, if I want to find a friend in a crowd, I will tune out other familiar faces and only see the one I'm looking for. Internally, our process works the same way. Our intentions are partly conscious, driven by conscious needs and wants, but many of them may be more unconscious. Our past experiences and memories stored in the body of our unconscious influence our conscious intentions in the present. We feel a strong urge, the desire to do, to act, to express. But so often if we stop and look at what the drive is underneath our feeling of action, it's hard to pinpoint its source. We feel much of our conscious intent as an impulse and a feeling.

The roots of our impulses are not conscious. Even if they were partially conscious, they wouldn't be entirely logical or rational. As we start validating the non-cognitive and non-rational parts of ourselves, we get more in touch with these subtle, tacit levels of intention. You may have experienced these levels of intention in the last exercise when you perceived something that was not physically related to the object you were visioning. When your awareness wanders or moves in an unexpected direction, remember to validate that movement. Your awareness may be following another, deeper level of intention.

I believe we have much less influence over our intentions than we would like to claim. Our deeper intentions arise out of the whole summation of who we are— our physical and non-physical, conscious and unconscious parts. It can be hard to quickly manifest a new reality when you want to change your life. You may consciously want to change, but unless your deeper intentions are also aligned with what you consciously desire, you may experience frustration or resistance to the changes.

As you pay attention, each intuitive exercise helps to reveal what your deeper intentions really are. By observing the action of your whole being - consciousness, mind, body, heart, all of you - you allow your deeper unconscious intentions to reveal themselves. When you notice you are experiencing something that isn't relevant to your conscious intent, it is probably relevant to some deeper intention you have. These deeper intentions may arise as a headache or a hot flash in the physical body, a strong emotion or a series of mental images and memories. When you allow these movements into your awareness and let yourself see where they lead, your conscious intention becomes more integrated with the intentions of your whole being.

Intention and Perception

Intention is intimately connected to what we perceive as well as our sense of self. Below is a diagram representing the three components. Intention, sense of self, and perception form a loop. Let's use the example of going to the refrigerator.

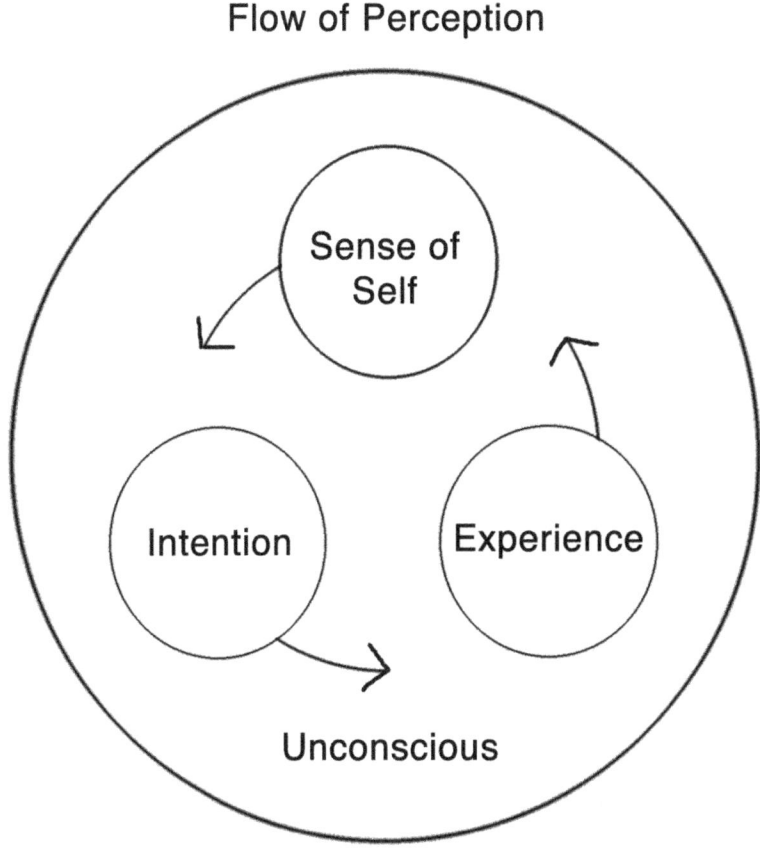

Figure 10

As this diagram illustrates, our intention leads us to what we experience and has an effect on how we experience the world. What we experience has an effect on our sense of who we are. We are modified by our experiences. Then our new, slightly changed sense of self directs our slightly adapted intention. We move through a cyclical process and all three elements change over time.

Think of what happens when we need to eat. Before we get hungry, we're doing whatever we're doing, being ourselves. Then an intention arises in the body, a feeling of hunger. This feeling moves us to go to the refrigerator and find some food. We experience that food, taste it, enjoy it and bring it into our body and mind, thus changing our sense of self. We are temporarily satisfied and now feel different intentions leading to different experiences.

This model illustrates a logical, linear view of consciousness; each part is isolated and discrete. They affect one another in a series. Focusing on these three aspects overshadows the rest of the circle, which contains all the other unconscious elements of being. Also in the unconscious are qualities of self, intention and experience of which we are not aware.

With direct perception, and the immersion of consciousness into present moment experience, the model changes significantly. (See figure 11 on the next page.) Self, intent, and experience blend together to form a larger Self in experience. The separate parts of self, intention and experience may only remain as faint memories compared to the living present. What we experience, how we intend, and who we are blends into the larger unconscious parts of what we are.

In immersed awareness, the quality of what we perceive changes dramatically. Our perceptions are similar to those we might have in a peak experience. We may have no sense of separation from the objects of our sensing. In direct, immersed perception, our experience becomes a spontaneous flow in the moment. The power of being "in the now" manifests. We experience a tremendous amount of meaning, even though, at the moment, we may have no conscious framework to process our experience.

Chapter 10 127

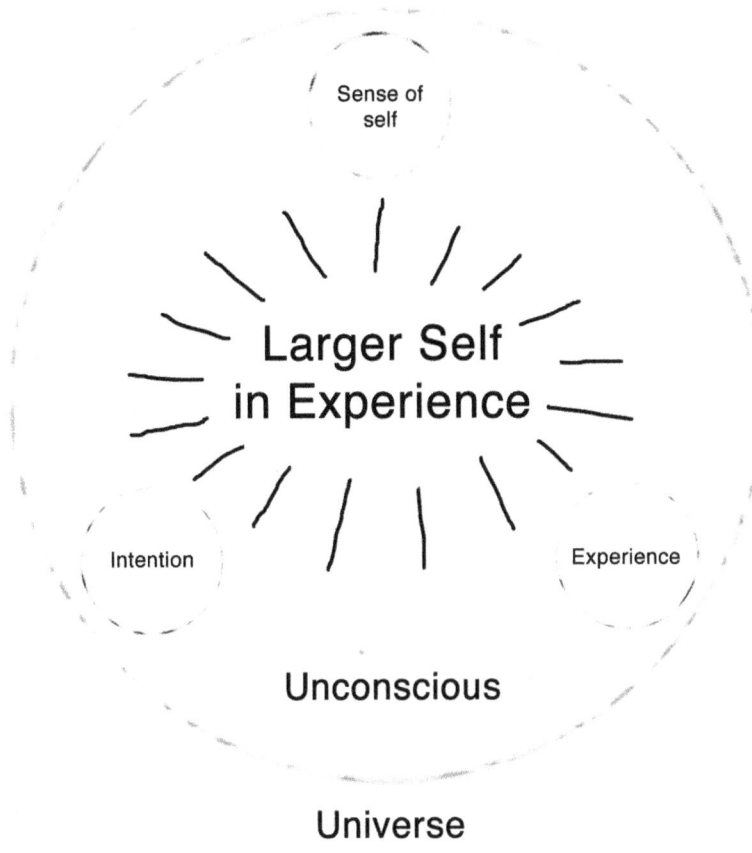

Figure 11

The immersed perception figure represents a peak or expanded experience where we are fully engaged in the present and not limited by our usual sense of self. When we are immersed in this way, we stop identifying with personal beliefs and may experience a strikingly different reality. Our unconscious, and higher consciousness aspects, have a stronger influence on our intention, our experience, as well as our sense of self.

We may return from a peak experience more aligned with our higher self and less conflicted. We may feel a greater sense of purpose. The sense of self we come back to may be much different than where we were oriented before the peak experience.

Unless we train ourselves to go there, full immersion only happens on rare occasions. More often, we move in small degrees towards the center of the diagram as we're cycling through intention, sensation and identity and only experience fully immersed knowing for brief moments.

An important aspect of an immersed experience is that the objective world is experienced as connected to oneself. It's accessed through the unconscious, but in consciousness, in the now. In that immersion, we are inseparable from what we perceive. This is why in the Immersed Perception diagram, even the outer circle is less distinct. Developing intuition leads to more awareness of that connection. Through the exercises in this book you have an opportunity to move your consciousness towards that connected experience. Every exercise is an opportunity to experience yourself in an expanded way. As you bring your awareness fully into each moment, you discover more unconscious aspects of yourself.

So you could ask yourself;

Why am I here?
What is my deeper purpose?

How is my present experience illuminating this deeper part of myself?

By asking these questions now, you point your awareness towards your deeper intentions. You can bring these subconscious levels into awareness by being open and receptive to what you are experiencing wherever you are. With intention, you can move gently towards the center of your self. There are many different intentions directing you at any moment. You have conscious concerns, physical body needs, even movements of your emotional body. You have also embodied the intentions of your spirit, your culture, your family, and perhaps even the intentions of the planet.

The more I explore my own awareness and intuition, the more I feel a greater desire to nurture an intimate loving relationship with my deepest sense self. My deepest self extends outward to my immediate environment, to the living communities around me, and even to the earth. Listening to the intentions of my deepest self allows me to serve the largest parts of my being. I sense spirit inside me and around me through the intimate sensual connection I have to the living world. I remember to breathe, come into my body, and attend to what I am experiencing.

> *What are you sensing now?*
> *Describe it.*

> *What meaningfulness is manifesting right now, through your present experience?*

Chapter 11

"There is also, of course, one's internal mapless country—what John Muir's biographer Michael Cohen calls the pathless way. Toward this I navigate. It cannot be helped. It is the way of mind and spirit leading to the most intriguing, most powerful landscape of all."
- Jim Dale Vickery

Clear Intent

You may sense your deeper intentions as a fascination, an emotional upwelling, even an unspeakable knowing. When your conscious focus is congruent and aligned with your deeper intention, you have what I call clear intent. Then all the parts of you can resonate together and you may experience a synchronistic flow in your life.

Can you sense the underlying intentions inside you?
Is there any direction bubbling up inside you?
Is there anything you might wish to respond to now?

Soften your eyes and make your mind more receptive. Read the following paragraphs slowly.

Inhale deeply now and fill your lungs.
Then purse your lips as if you had a straw in your mouth and exhale all the air through that straw until you're lungs are empty.
Repeat this deep breath a few times.
Enjoy the feeling of the air passing in and out of you.
Allow your breathing to relax and settle into a comfortable rhythm.
Become aware of what you are experiencing now.

What are you sensing?
What are you feeling?

As you become more present, you are tuning into the intentions of a deeper part of yourself.
What is arising within you is your internal wisdom becoming conscious.
The fullness of your present experience brings you into clearer intent.

Imagine that you could allow this upwelling intention to guide you.
Where does it take you?
What comes to mind?

Give your self some time now to explore your inner guidance.

Gently allow your conscious mind to become more active.
Describe what you are sensing.
Write down your thoughts and feelings.
Draw what you are sensing.

When you're ready, activate your body again.

Stand up and stretch.
Take a refreshing breath and become more aware of the space around you.

If your conscious intent is directed towards experiencing intuition, health or wholeness, and it resonates with your deeper intentions, then you will experience these things. The clearer your intention, the easier it comes. There are openings for becoming that which you wish to be in every moment. Present and future merge in this moment as consciousness unfolding. This is clear intent.

> *Take another moment now and remember a time when you felt a clarity about yourself and your life.*
>
> *Bring that memory to mind now.*
> *Enjoy it.*
> *Remember what was happening to you, in you, and around you.*
> *Remember the feeling of that clarity and that flow.*
>
> *Then, describe it to yourself.*

When your conscious focus is aligned with your deeper intentions, there is less resistance in the mind/body system. A trained intuitive, artist or visionary can go directly to the target they seek. With experience, they've learned to ask and expect the information they seek. They've also practiced enough so that most of their unconscious parts are aligned with their conscious intent. Intuition has become a process that they've integrated into who they are, a larger part of their lives that extends beyond the exercise at hand. When it flows easily, there are few unresolved belief conflicts in their unconscious.

Knowing, "Why am I here?" or "Why am I doing this?" is important, even while you're doing a simple exercise like a body focus. Initially, you may not know exactly what you are seeking. You may know in your conscious mind why you are reading this book, but there may also be other, deeper intentions. Cultivating clear intention thus is a process of self-discovery, of staying present to learn about yourself. You may also become aware you have other important intentions, such as: "to live more artfully," or "to come from the source," or perhaps "to be more loving." Cultivating intuition will move you towards those goals.

Allowing

If you've lived your life predominantly in your conscious mind, in cognitive processing, then the deeper intentions arising from within you may be difficult to attend to. You may only sense wisps—airy, slight movements, or obscure feelings. However subtle they are, you can still attend to them. With attention, they will become clearer because you will attend to yourself with softness, gentleness and appreciation.

Allowing is similar to the phenomena of resonance in sound. When you strike a bell, it sends its sound out into space. When that energy hits another similar bell, it starts vibrating as well. The second bell embodies the energy of the first bell. It takes no effort for the second bell to sound. It happens spontaneously as the energy passes through it.

In the same way, all you have to do is allow your body/mind to respond. You choose to stay with not knowing or not understanding as those first vibrations begin to set you into motion. You don't know what sound will occur as it's beginning. You may perceive a tingling or an itch. But as it becomes stronger, the sound begins to manifest. As you allow it to manifest, you experience meaning and understanding. You relax into it and allow it.

This kind of perception has conscious and unconscious elements. You recognize the beginnings of a change, as you come to some kind of threshold and you relax into it. The many methods of seeking an intuitive awareness have conscious elements and protocols, but they all, in some way, bridge both conscious and subconscious states. Every awareness practice builds a similar bridge. Your intention carries you up to the threshold, and then, in that moment, you are in the present, receptive, and not knowing. The flow of energy and information can move through your unconscious into your conscious experience. Rhea White, the editor of the journal "Exceptional Human Experience", describes this balancing:

> *"Unconsciously, however, and without effort, one may be oriented toward events with which our normal perception is unable to make contact, and if this orientation is strongly motivated, contact may be established in another way - subconsciously - provided only that the conscious processes do not interfere.* [34]

The exercises in sensory awareness, receptivity and allowing teach us to get the conscious mind out of the way. Intuitive information comes through this gentle balancing between expression of intention with its release and the openness to the next arriving unknown. Also, as White says, when the intentions are subconscious, we may only be aware of the receiving of something important and not see any conscious connection to our intentions and efforts.

You can practice the presence of being in the moment with tools like the mandala and the breath. You can put yourself in the right position, with intent and expectancy, and also with willingness and receptivity. Being present with all of yourself, including your physical body, allows those messages from your unconscious to manifest. A great way to see the intentions of the past is to be present now in your experience. You are already receiving feedback.

> *Your experience now, in this moment, is already the response of your previous intentions. Imagine that.*
> *What information is your present experience providing you that relates to your deeper intentions?*

Allowing Intuition - Target

Now you will shift back to present awareness and away from cognitive processes. For this next exercise you can read and experience as you go, or you could find a friend to read the following text to you. You will need internet access for the feedback for this target. Refer to Appendix A on page 287 if you don't have internet access and would like to create your own target for this exercise.

Take a moment now and come into your breath...
Then sense what is inside you...

Describe what you are experiencing.

Notice how what you sense changes as you shift your focus from thinking to sensing. Some part of you has deemed every sensation and awareness within you worthy of your attention. Your experience of yourself now is the result of your conscious and unconscious intentions.
You don't have to do anything.
You can just BE for a few moments and feel yourself shift.

Now bring in an intent to access intuition.
From there, in the same way you do a body focus, you continue to observe whatever comes into your awareness.

Then ask yourself,
"What is the target?"
or say,
"I want to perceive the target Patrick has chosen now."

Then wait and observe.
You don't have to make anything happen.

Imagine being suspended, waiting, like the gull in the wind,
 holding your intent, being present, allowing and observing.

Give yourself time.
You may turn away from these words and go deeper.

Or continue reading with soft eyes and mind and be guided.

Anything you experience now is in some way your response to

the target—any color, shape, sound, texture—anything at all.
What do you perceive?
As you notice changes in imagery, feeling, emotions, sounds, or anything at all, just pay attention.
Observe and allow without needing to respond in any particular way.
Just pay attention.
Allow yourself to be with an unknown sense or a change until it resolves all by itself.

How would you describe your perceptions?
Put a few words to them.
Draw.

You can describe your experience, as it is, without needing to place it into a context or a meaning.
As you describe your experiences, what you are sensing will change.
When you notice changes, continue describing, allowing and watching.

What are you experiencing now?
Note it again...
and again...

Be honest and do your best to be descriptive with your words.
Wait, watch, learn to stay with your intent to be present.
Be at the balance point, hovering.

As soon as you are clear, as the word and thought in your mind matches your experience, then it will move or shift or change in some way.
Until it reaches that clarity, allow it to be an unknown.
Stay with it.

If you want to go further, you can do the same thing again

without reading.
Repeat the question... "What is the target?"
Then follow your own process.
You can do it now.

When you're done write "End" on your paper. Let yourself disconnect with your stream. Let your intent shift back to your conscious self.

Then remember, you can take care of yourself.
Is there anything you need to do now to attend to your deeper intentions?

Each time you approach an exercise similar to this one, you can take as long as you like, the time that feels right to you. If you sense you want to go further with it, then relax, let it go longer, extend your receptivity. You can draw, write, speak, and even move in some way that allows you to stay with what you are sensing. Writing or describing your experience, especially at these early stages is essential. Writing and describing builds the bridge between conscious thought and non-conscious processes. You are allowing your meaning to become conscious.

Every time you move into the flow of sensing, receiving and describing, you build a bridge to other states of consciousness more directly connected to larger parts of yourself. With familiarity, much more information can be transferred between these different states of consciousness.

Target Feedback

Now you can get your feedback. You can view the target feedback online now at www.AJoyfulIntuition.com/Target2.jpg. If you created your own target, you can open the envelope and view the picture now.

Then continue reading below.

Keep in mind the target was actually what is pictured in the photo, and not just the photo. You may have had full sensory responses. You may also have perceived information not contained in the photo.

When you look at the photo, your conscious mind will immediately come up with a response. It may want to take control again and come up with a label or a judgment about what you just experienced. Rather than believing what your conscious mind says, you have a choice. You can take a moment to integrate your feedback.

Take a moment and breathe.
Notice your reaction to the photo.
What is your first response?
Pay attention to it.
Describe it.

Are you happy? Sad? Indifferent? Curious? Other feelings?
Describe your feeling and any insights as to why these feelings are there.
Then engage your awareness with that target using all your senses.
Describe what you perceive with each sense.
Describe where it takes you.
You can even include a description of how your experience may have flowed outside of words and ideas.

Is there a feeling response to this target?
How does your body respond?

Sketch the basic elements of your feedback.
Then, after you've become more receptive again, go back and compare the target with your intuitive responses.
Notice any associations, similarities, connections, resonances.

Circle anything that feels like a connection to you.
Take notes about how the process worked for you.

Do it now.

Shifting into receptivity for your feedback is an important step. It's very easy to become critical or self-judgmental when you get feedback. Regardless of how "good" you did, a critical mental attitude will limit your learning. Shifting back to sensing allows you to access deeper learnings and intentions. It allows you to see beyond the specifics of a single exercise to the larger framework of your learning.

Each intuitive exercise you do is an exercise in awareness. It's OK to want to judge how well you did, but with a shift to sensing again you can balance your mental desire to quantify your experience with your deeper intentions to expand your awareness. You can be present with yourself as you get feedback.

More on Feedback

As you practice allowing and sensing, you will begin to sense when you are more present and less in your mind. As you receive feedback, you can consciously recognize the accuracies and the moments of connection and flow. You will learn to trust yourself more. The more familiar you become with your own process, the less you need external feedback. Then you can trust your own sense of "rightness" in the moment.

Your feedback will also help you see how your mind works. After describing several perceptions did your mind start telling you what it was? Did an image or sensation remind you of an experience you had? In some remote viewing protocols the activation of the conscious mind is called an Analytical Overlay (AOL). Anytime your mind jumps in and starts putting things together or reaching conclusions, you're in AOL. When you notice it happening, just write what your mind came up with and write "mind" or "AOL" next to it. That way you put it in its place. You recognize how your mind works, and you don't have to fight it.

For example, if you perceived blue, or blue-green, hard, and flat, what do you think you would be describing? What first comes to mind for me is a plastic swimming pool. If I recognized that it was my mind that came up with the label I would write, "AOL - plastic swimming pool." Acknowledging it allows me to clear the thought while it's happening. Then I shift back to receptivity and continue.

When you get feedback you will also recognize how and when your mind jumped in. You might see that the blue-green color and the hard, flat texture were related to the target, which wasn't a swimming pool.

When you get feedback to an exercise, one sense might grab you first. It could be the shape, texture, emotion, or purpose of the target. Notice what grabs you, since in your intuitive process you may have a tendency to respond in much the same way.

Again, this is an example of deeper intentions; certain senses or qualities are more meaningful to you. You may also notice that certain senses are consistently more accurate. If you have one sense that is more accurate, then you can work with it in your intuitive process. Try focusing first on that sense when you let go of your intent. Then let your awareness flow outward from there to other senses.

Often, when I walk into a room, I check in first with my physical sensations. After that I may begin to notice smells in the room, or visual information, or even my emotional response. Often the flow of my intuitive sensing moves through the same progression. With attention and practice, you can notice the flow that works well for you.

I want to take a moment to stress the importance of following through this entire cycle of awareness with each intuitive exercise you do. Begin with intent, flow into perception, and go all the way through to feedback and self-reflection. Each part of the cycle helps you learn about yourself.

Intuitive Process

The Following diagram and explanation reviews the entire sequence to use for each exercise:

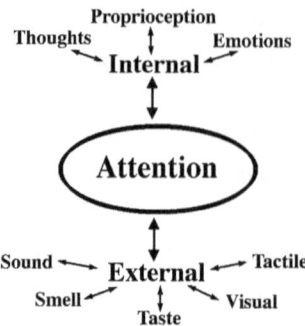

1 - Have a target or intuitive exercise prepared where you can get feedback.

2 - Do a body focus. Use the attention figure above as a guide. Be aware of all the channels of information you already have access to. Describe what you are already sensing or experiencing in any of these channels.

The body focus allows a clearing of those channels so you can be more present. If you are experiencing a strong emotion or physical sensation, you may want to describe it in more detail. Then wait until you can be fully present in a calm, receptive way.

3 - Take a moment and do whatever else you need to do to put yourself in a state conducive to accessing your intuition. You can relax more, meditate, clear your mind or even go for a walk. Take as much time as you need. Then when you're ready...

4 - State your intent to access the target. You might say something like "I want perceptions of what is in the envelope to be presented to my consciousness."

5 - Become receptive and wait for perceptions or changes to appear.

6 - Sketch or describe any and all perceptions and awarenesses you have. If you come up with labeling phrases such as a "watch" or a "chair," you can write them down as an AOL. Then ask your-

self, "What made me think of a ... (watch or chair, etc.)?" Take yourself back to direct perceptions. You can allow unknown sensations to resolve at their own pace. You don't have to do anything to make it happen.

At any point during this phase, you can direct your awareness with specific questions, such as "Are there any colors?" or "Is it old?" After questioning, remain receptive and wait for information to arrive in ANY of your senses. Just because you ask for a color doesn't mean that will be your next perception.

Stay in the flow of perceiving and describing until you feel you are done.

7 - Write "End" somewhere after your descriptions. You are setting up a ritual of closing your psychic space so you can ground again into the present.

8 - Then notice if any of the information you described has any meaning to you. If it does, describe it. At this stage, you can use the intelligence and reasoning of your conscious mind. It is a valuable tool. Be aware though, you may not have enough information to conclude anything.

9 - Get your feedback. If your feedback is delayed, then wait until you have feedback to continue with the process.

10 - With feedback, describe your initial reaction to your feedback—thoughts, feelings, and impressions.

11 - Now engage your senses with the feedback. Describe your perceptions of the actual target here. Notice what grabs your attention first and start there. Try to use all your senses. Also sketch the target or significant parts of it. Remember, it doesn't matter how "good" you are. The act of sketching, even basic images, activates the non-logical parts of your brain.

12 - Now refer back to your intuitive perceptions from step #6. Circle anything that seems to be associated with the target. You can

allow yourself some leeway here. It's your feeling that's most important. As you progress in your abilities and confidence, you can be more critical and circle only information that is clearly apparent in the feedback.

13 - Afterwards, take a minute to answer each of these questions:

How do you feel about your perceptions for this target?

Is that feeling different than your initial reaction at #10 above?

Were there any perceptions you forgot to put on the paper?

Describe any insights or understandings about your awareness or intuition from this exercise?

What could you do differently next time you do an intuitive exercise?

You can use this process every time you do an exercise. As you're learning to trust your intuition, be sure to pick targets where you will get feedback. If you want to do another picture target like this one, you can. In Appendix A I explain how to create your own targets or use the web site www.rvtargets.com for targets. Also in Appendix B there are more internet sites listed with practice targets. Many remote viewing trainers have practice targets available online.

One way to sense this expectancy is to imagine you're standing on a stage in bright lights. Up above you past the light is darkness. Then imagine throwing a tennis ball up in the air into the dark. Once it disappears you wait, watch and observe. You know it will come down eventually, so you wait. That is the same feeling you may feel in the intuitive process. You release your intent and wait for the response. You may get a response quickly or slowly, but something will come to you. You don't have to reach for it.

What you receive may be something totally different than what you threw in the air. That's part of the adventure.

When you're done with your on-line target and you want feedback, turn on the computer and click on the number to view your feedback picture. Then finish the steps in the form.

Another way to do practice targets is to have a friend make them up for you. At the beginning, tell them to use pictures that have one clear, central focus as a target. They can glue them to a piece of paper so you won't see, and possibly get confused by the pictures on the back. If they make ten or twelve of these, you'll have your own target pool to practice with.

As you continue in this book you will find many other kinds of exercises you can do. Whatever ones you enjoy, do them again. You can do as many as you want and enjoy your learning. But make sure and take care of yourself too. It takes energy to learn to shift your attention and awareness. So when your body tells you it needs a break, listen to it. Remember you are building a relationship with a larger part of your being, and the process of learning and expanding is what it's all about.

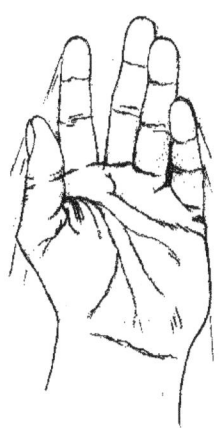

Chapter 12

Unconscious Messaging

When you do a target, the flow of your awareness may guide you to information that is personal. When you review your feedback, you may think this information is just wrong. Everything you experience has meaning, though that meaning may be unconscious. The same is true for the body focus. To your conscious mind, what you describe in the moment may only illuminate your perceptive abilities or the nature of your thought processes. At a deeper level you are constructing elegant interconnections between states of consciousness, between the mind and the body, and even between your sense of self and the rest of the world.

Every time you extend your intent into the subtle inner realms and validate what you experience, the connections inside you become stronger.

> *How is your body now?*
> *Are there other intentions manifesting?*
> *Do you need to stretch, move, or breathe?*
> *Do you need a drink of water?*
> *You can attend to those distractions.*
> *You can validate the messages from your unconscious.*

I sincerely hope you do respond to other parts of your being when they manifest. Things that distract your focus may be the outward movements of deeper-seated intentions. A sore back can be attended to. You can stretch, breathe or just pay attention. Consider engaging with these body messages in other ways, as if they were an intelligence, or a voice speaking in a different language.

What is that sensation saying?
Can you listen to it?
Can you allow it into your awareness and follow its directives?

A sensation showing up in your body can be intuitive as well. It may provide you with direct, tangible information. For example if you have a sore back every time you are with a person. If you pay attention to that sensation, your body may be telling you something else about you or the other person. A sensation in your body may not always translate simply saying, "This is safe" or "Don't date them." It may mean something more subtle, "Here, is a doorway to spirit - a direct connection. Pay attention. Be aware."

There is a subtle, intuitive messaging always alive inside you.

As you trust yourself, more and more, your inner prompting may even move you into a spontaneous physical movement, one that doesn't even make sense. Eventually you may find true value. I've known people who give gifts with this kind of inner trust. They have no conscious idea why a certain gift should go to a certain person. But they trust it. The receiver of the gift may say how synchronistic it was to get it just then. This reaction confirms the giver's intuition to give it. Other times they get no feedback at all, but they still trust their gift-giving urge.

You can be present with whatever flows through you without any expectations of results.
What is manifesting within you now?

Reaching out with Intuition

So here's another exercise with feedback. Read this exercise through first, and then do it.

Start with a brief body focus.

Take two or three deep, relaxing breaths.
Tune into your senses.
What colors do you see?
Sounds?
Smells?
What you are feeling?
Are you warm?
Are you feeling any emotions?

Observe what you are experiencing mentally and emotionally.

Describe these senses.

If you feel a need to respond in some way to what you're sensing, do so.

Remember a conversation you had recently with a close friend.
Remember the sound of her voice, phrases she used, and your feelings when talking with her.

You connect to this person through these memories.
You begin to resonate with them in the present.

Now ask yourself a question;

Is she home? Is she at work? Is she feeling happy, sad, etc. Ask yourself questions you don't know the answer to.
After asking, wait for an answer.

Notice anything you experience after you ask the question and write it down.

Pay attention to your first perceptions.

Ask another question.
Remember to be respectful of her privacy.
Don't ask a question you wouldn't ask your friend in person.

Release the question and wait for the answer.
Write down all your perceptions, feelings, even thoughts while this is happening.
It's all part of the flow of this exercise.

Is there anything else you want to know?

Ask as many questions as you want, noticing any perceptions you have for each question.

Pay attention to your responses.
Write them down.

After asking all the questions you want, check in with yourself again.

Has anything else changed in you?
Describe that.

Do the exercise now.

After you're finished, call your friend.
Share with her what you're doing.
Ask your questions.
Be aware how you feel as you get your feedback.
You are in an intuitive process and learning about yourself.

What responses do you have as you get your feedback?
Write them down. Take notes. Remember, you're learning.
Thank her for helping you with your exploration.

When you're done with your conversation, go back to your list. Circle the answers you feel were intuitive perceptions. Remember the sensations you had for the these answers. Was there any consistency? How about the ones that didn't seem related to the feedback?

This exercise is a nice example of directly applying intuition. There are unlimited ways to make intuition practical. Any time you are going to get information by regular methods, you can check your intuition first. Ask, pay attention, and note your results. Then get your feedback. Every new experience becomes part of your learning.

In fact, any time you experience a change, you can be more open to the possibility of intuitive sensitivity. What happens when you enter into that person's house? Describe it? Does it have meaning to you?

What happens when you're at work and you get a pleasant sense that reminds you of another friend? Do you imagine they're thinking about you? Call them and see. Unless you ask, you'll miss the opportunity to validate your intuition. What's the worst that could happen? If they weren't thinking of you, tell them you were thinking of them. Your energy extends to them and may even change their day in a positive way. That may have been the reason the thought came into your mind in the first place.

> Using your intuition doesn't replace your ability to think rationally. It just augments it and balances it. Intuition is intimately connected with reason.

When you trust your intuition, you activate a personal intelligence and wisdom that can be deeply meaningful and fulfilling. Using your intuition doesn't replace your ability to think rationally. It just augments it and balances it. Intuition is intimately connected with reason. You can be very logical and highly intuitive at the same time. You may experience a slight shift in your awareness while talking with a friend or walking to work. Paying attention to that information may enrich the quality of your present experience and your work day.

> *Imagine having an unconscious ally who's aligning every conscious experience with the manifestation of your deepest intentions.*
>
> *Can you be open and receptive to those influences?*

Chapter 13

Description Releases

Each time we can recognize something, it frees it up to move. This is true for intuitive information as well as for emotional or physical changes. Then if there is more we need to know or more we need to do, the next piece will come all by itself. All we need to do is be conscious and receptive.

For example, as I'm settling in with a check-in, I may feel a pressure in my chest. As I feel into it, my awareness opens and more comes. Along with the feeling of pressure, I now sense a feeling of heaviness, which then feels more sad. I name it, "I'm feeling sadness." At this I remember someone I thought of earlier in the day, whom I now realize I miss. As I feel this, the sadness starts to pass, I feel appreciation for them, and I feel a desire to connect with them. Now the pressure is gone, the sadness is gone and I'm feeling more present with myself.

Now if I'd glossed over the initial feeling of pressure in my intent to do an intuitive exercises, then that underlying subconscious intention would have interfered with my conscious intentions, and my perceptions might not have been as clear.

The more I practice being present in the flow of the moment, the more I realize the meaning in my life comes from this alive presence. The meaning does not come from any particular content I desire or encounter. I may be focused on one particular idea or object, but in holding on to the wanting, I pull myself out of the flow of actually receiving it. What I am experiencing is already leading me towards what is important to me. I only have to trust it. When I allow my awareness to go into a newly arriving perception, I let go of what I previously thought was me. In doing so, I step out of the known and move back into being. The new sense is actually me in formation. My present moment experience is more congruent as an evolving, dynamic consciousness than any concrete idea or object I can focus on.

As you practice being present with yourself and the flow of your awareness, you will discover yourself to be more than just what you're sensing. As you resonate with deeper levels of your own intention, any phenomena you experience, positive or negative, becomes part of your process and thus, easier to move through.

Our expectations about how we want things to be can obscure the meaning that is already manifesting. Expectation is looking towards the future for something in the past. We even develop expectations about what the next letting go will be like. But, in the next moment, even letting go may manifest in a completely different way. Your letting go in this moment may lead you to a momentary breath, connecting you with your unconscious, or it may become a complete break into a nap or a walk. Letting go and allowing can become doing or not doing, being or not being, or even something wholly outside language. You don't know until you let go of expectation, attend, and respond to what is arising within you right in the moment.

You may wonder, if you are completely open to the moment, how you can get anything done. You might wonder if your sensorium would then just completely occupy your awareness. I haven't found this to be true.

You are drawn in your own perfect way into the next moment and the next experience. Most of the information flowing through your senses doesn't even impact your conscious awareness. Your intention is always guiding you at a deeper level. If there is information that is relevant to you, then it will arise into your consciousness as part of your being present. Thus when you are distracted by something, there may be meaning in that movement. What distracts you may be bringing you a new piece of information helping you to shift your state of mind. If you find yourself focusing on a task or a goal again, that's OK too. You are expressing your intention and what is important to you.

You obviously do not have to seek distractions in order to access your deeper intentions. You are already being guided by a larger part of you. Sensations that arise in your awareness will either fade away on their own or get stronger. When they get stronger, there is more information within them. The message will come all by itself as you open and stay present. When a sensation fades away, it has no more personal meaning for you at that moment. You can go elsewhere with your attention. Your deeper intentions guide the flow of your present moment experience.

> **What distracts you may be bringing you a new piece of information helping you to shift your state of mind.**

For example, I glance at a picture of a jaguar in a magazine. Then I notice I am feeling a warmth in my chest and I feel happier. I stop to acknowledge my reactions and my body responds more, my breathing shifts, and my state of mind becomes calmer. Then, as I sit with these sensations and insights, nothing else comes. I feel drawn to go back to reading.

So what's the meaning of this experience? There doesn't seem to be anything else intuitive about the picture of the cat. If there were, then more would have come as I stayed present with myself. What I know is what I've experienced. When I saw the photo, I felt a shift. I feel a little more connected with myself and balanced as I go back to reading. There may be more for me to learn, but for now, that's it.

> *When you need rest and balancing, your unconscious will lead you to that.*
> *Are there senses or places you like to go that help you connect*

> *with yourself?*
> *How do you recognize these places?*

Personal Needs

As you begin to open yourself to other kinds of information, it is important to stay connected with yourself, and to stay in touch with your physical, mental and emotional needs. This is why the Body Focus is important. It helps you pay attention to those needs. You can also learn what helps you connect with yourself.

For example, I love walking in nature. I'm fortunate to live close to the mountains and I can easily go for walks. When I walk a physical path through the natural landscape, I also step into my inner path of congruence and clarity. Sometimes when I start walking I feel very disconnected with myself and with the land. My thoughts might be jumbled. I might not be very conscious of my body. Yet with each step I take, my attention begins to flow out into the environment and into what is happening in my body. I gradually feel a sense of release and letting go. I shift from a place of some internal disconnect into a more balanced, whole-being awareness.

On these walks I often gain insight into problems I've been having. My emotions become clearer and calmer, and I am able to think well. I recognize the state I move into when I'm walking as a state of clear intent. My whole awareness becomes more responsive to everything I encounter, more intuitive. My energy flows from that connected feeling into ideas, goals, and desires, while deepening my connection to the present.

Referring back to the immersed awareness figure on page 127, when my conscious self extends into the landscape, I move into a greater state of flow and my unconscious resources become more accessible. I have a more clear perspective of my life and my intentions. I get a clearer sense of where my life is moving, while being strongly grounded in the physical present. Clear intent isn't just an idea or an image in my mind, or a distant goal to be attained. It is an extension of living fully in the present. Expectation, on the other hand, has a sense of pressure, of needing something, of not being entirely with myself in the moment.

Aligning to my self in this flowing way reminds me of improvisation. Learning the fundamentals of a skill or of an instrument. You spend a lot of time in practice. Over time, the mechanics of playing the instrument shifts over to the subconscious. Your conscious awareness can respond to other creative impulses and flow with them. Like a musical skill, all the sensory awareness and allowing practices you are learning, through this book's intuitive exercises, become the foundation for you. You will have more ability to respond spontaneously and creatively in the moment. Then, being more present and in the flow, you can sense a subtle shift in your body while you're shaking someone's hand, and enjoying that gift, you learn from it.

Your awareness flows with all the energies you experience and you become more able to respond consciously. The flow of the moment becomes a marriage of mind, heart and body, with many conscious and unconscious forces. Living improvisationally comes from a balance between allowing and doing. You embody your clear intentions by living within your own aliveness. You will trust when you are "On" more and more. You will know you are in a changing flow of your own unfolding.

Future Sensing

I'd like you to focus on yourself again for a few moments, using your imagination, your memory and your intuition.

> *Bring to mind a time or a place when you felt connected with yourself.*
> *Wherever that was, let yourself remember the senses of that experience—the smells, sounds, images, tastes, sensations on your body or in your body. Remember the emotions and the thoughts flowing through you.*
> *Let your body remember and enjoy all the sensations.*
>
> *Take a few moments and breathe into those feelings.*
> *Relax into yourself.*
>
> *As you enjoy these feelings, notice how they affect you now.*

You are giving yourself a gift.
As you remember this experience, you may remember other times, other places when you felt similar, meaningful feelings and sensations.
You can enjoy those connections too. You can enjoy the inner, guided flow of your own remembering.

Then from here, imagine letting this feeling sense carry you forward into future experiences.
Is there something you would do, perhaps some activity, that you would deeply enjoy, that would also ground you and connect you to your deepest sense of self?
Imagine doing that now, or being there.
Would there be other people, beings, or animals there?

As you imagine, allow whatever feelings and experiences arise.
Your body may relax now.
Your body may move.

Use your senses.
Take your time.
Make it vivid in your awareness.

Enjoy that letting go and allow your imagining to guide you.
Enjoy what you experience and deepen your connection to your evolving self.

Then, after enjoying your visioning as much as you'd like.
Describe all of what you are experiencing.
Translate your experience into drawing or language.
Build that bridge within yourself.
Be clear and concise.

And if you need more, you can go now and do what you were imagining.

After imagining in this way, you may realize you would like more of this sense of being "On". If you like it, you can take steps to actually feel this way more. You can take more time envisioning it. Maybe there's an activity you can do. Perhaps there's a special place you can actually go. You could climb your mountain, dance, run, laugh, sing, move into your art, or do whatever connects you to yourself.

Listen to what your inner self wants.
Sense the intention that speaks to your conscious mind from a deeper level.
Attend to yourself.
Allow yourself to go where you need to go.

When I am physically engaging with a landscape, I have a connection to my clear intent. I am grateful I have learned to recognize this state. As you pay attention to yourself, you will recognize when you are connected. You already have your own ways to do this, and perhaps several ways. You will become more aware of these connective self-expressions as you validate your feelings and respond consciously to what is alive in you.

Redefining Noise

Following your intuitive path, you may experience totally irrelevant material not connected to your conscious intentions. Say you're attempting to intuitively perceive a practice target, and you perceive sadness. When you discover that the target was an apple, you can see no connection to the sadness. This kind of seemingly irrelevant information can be called noise, or static. Noise then refers to perceptions that have no obvious connection to the target, much like static occurring on a TV or radio transmission.

This noise though, in your intuitive context, may be personally relevant. I always suggest that you record everything that comes in during an intuitive exercise. Even if you don't understand the meaning of something you are experiencing, your record will validate the intention of the deeper part of you that brought it into your awareness.

Here's an example of the value of noise. In the classes I teach, everyone brings a personal object to use as a target. We pair up and perceive each other's objects. One woman I worked with had an interesting response. The first perceptions she got were of candy. She perceived the size, shape, taste of the candy as well as the feeling of being a little girl. Her perceptions didn't have anything to do with the object that was in my pocket. She didn't know that of course, and just described it anyhow. After these first "candy" perceptions, she went on to accurately describe the little carved stone that was in my pocket. When I asked her about it afterwards, she remembered that her father used to surprise her with candies when she was a little girl. He'd pull them out of his pocket and give them to her.

Her initial perceptions were related to her own psyche. It may have been the focus on the pockets or the playfulness of the exercise that triggered her associations. I also had the sense that there was a sense of comfort being communicated by her unconscious. Her childlike side said, "Yes, it's OK to proceed. I feel safe." Her descriptions were not accurate perceptions of my target, but they were meaningful to her and to her process.

Every perception you have, either direct or intuitive, is filtered through your consciousness. The meaning of a particular perception may simply have to do with learning the process of intuition, of becoming aware or letting go. It may also relate to a belief or a concern that your unconscious is working out. It may relate to a past experience. It may also relate to the target you're wanting to perceive. Mapping out how your consciousness flows will help you sort out which information is personality, what is deeper soul or collective information, and what is related to a working target.

As you experience successes, you will start to think, "I can do this. I am intuitive." This acknowledgment sends ripples down into your unconscious. Beliefs are stretched or expanded. Other intentions then become more active, such as concerns about protection, stability and safety. These unconscious movements may start to interrupt your initial effortless flow, bringing more "noise" in your exercises. Every significant experience will contain these unconscious movements. It creates a ripple down effect that restructures your personal beliefs. As this happens, your unconscious guides the process. Something arises that distracts you and you feel a need to nap or walk. All of these movements allow integration and internal processing. If you continue doing the same intuitive exercises, your accuracy may go down for a little while, but you are still increasing your awareness and integrating.

Remember the feeling of learning and expanding...

If you let go and allow this noise while holding your intent to become intuitive, your accuracy will return. When noise appears, you recognize it as part of you, part of the process. Your subconscious is processing and learning too. To expand your intuitive abilities you may need to update your beliefs about what intuition is, and, more importantly, who you are. As you continue the practice, you will become more present in the moment. The more present you are, the more easily you will flow into your true potential.

To start using your intuition there is nothing extra needed, nothing else you need to gain. Explore your desire to learn, love it, and live it and you will clarify your intent. You will clear the channels of your perception. Intuition is already real for you now and can manifest even more. When conflicts arise between your beliefs and your experiences, you may feel tension in your body, mind, or heart. Staying present with that tension, describing it and making it conscious will allow it to move and release.

Stay present with what is in you.
You can open the doorway into the next experience.
Are there messages arising within you that need attention?

Pause...

You can remember and revisit things you enjoy.

Envision an object - You can exercise your inner awareness by envisioning an object you know. Your inner awareness can lead your awareness. You may even perceive in a new way. Get feedback.

Extend intent - Telephone - You can extend your inner awareness to anything you want to perceive. When you're going to call someone, ask yourself questions first. Use your inner sensitivity. Then get feedback.

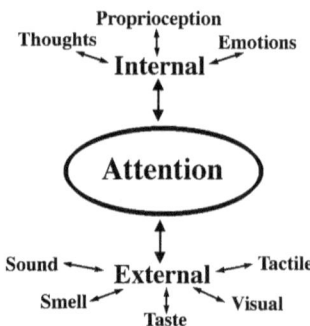

Body Focus - As an awareness practice, you can focus your attention into your body. This includes your extended body, your mind, heart and general state of being. Allow yourself to go into what you are experiencing. Enjoy. Then describe to yourself. Make yourself more present and integrated through the experience of the body.

Description Releases - Remember, when you acknowledge and describe your experience accurately, you release yourself from that experience. You move back into the flow of the moment.

Chapter 14

Fascination

What fascinates you? Do you notice when you are caught and absorbed by something fascinating? Do you respond? Following your fascination allows your awareness to move in non-logical ways. The sense of fascination will lead you into a present expression of your deeper intentions.

> *Bring to mind something that fascinates you.*
> *Are there feelings that come with fascination?*
> *Remember what it feels like to be drawn in and engaged with something.*
> *Allow your sense of fascination to stay with you as you continue reading.*

Feelings of fascination, wonder and awe come from deep within us. They are manifestations of unconscious intent. When I see a newborn baby, I feel a sense of awe and fascination. I see the miniature body fully formed in the human shape and am amazed. I can sense the life-force and intelligence already in this tiny being. I think how this intelligence is guided by something wholly outside of normal physical reality. The child evolved in the womb guided by a deeper intelligence.

When I see a baby and think about him, I come up against an edge inside me. I can't quite get my mind around the miracle of this creation, this life energy. I haven't had children and feel some sadness about my decision not to have children. At the same time, I feel such a fascination and aliveness when I see children. I am captivated. I perceive a beautiful majesty that I can't quite comprehend. Fascinations always have a connection to something larger than our conscious awareness. They are dreaming undercurrents that direct our conscious lives. There is more to my fascination about the newborn than my mental understanding. These fascinations are one of the means that the unconscious uses to make deeper intentions known.

> *Remember again a fascination you have experienced.*
> *Feel it in your body.*
>
> *Observe where it takes you, how it changes your awareness and your body.*
>
> *Then attend to the source of that sense.*
> *Where does it originate?*
>
> *Let your awareness deepen into that source.*
>
> *Any thoughts? Feelings? Physical sensations?*
> *After enjoying it, describe your perceptions to yourself.*

Remembering these feelings will draw more of what fascinates you into consciousness. You can pay attention to the subtle threads of attraction that are always flirting around the boundaries of your conscious awareness. You can follow those threads and move into a clearer relationship with your deeper, soulful self.

Charged Emotions

As you practice being more in your body in the present moment, you will be more able to stay with sensations that have high energy or emotional charge. These charged moments are often fertile opportunities for insight and growth. Whenever we experience stronger emotions, our awareness is less in the realm of conscious structures and more connected to the subconscious. They are experienced as more vivid and alive. We generally like the strong emotions we enjoy and struggle with the ones we don't like. Being in the body can help shift the resistance we have to these strong energies.

Anger has been a difficult emotion for me to acknowledge and be with. One time I awoke from a dream angry. I made a conscious effort to stay with the feeling. Underneath the anger, I was also feeling fear connected to strong sensations in my body. I felt a tightness and churning activity in the pit of my stomach. As I stayed with these sensations, I spontaneously shifted back and forth between the imagery I'd been experiencing in my dream and the feelings in my body. Somehow the two were connected.

In my dream, I was with a group of people walking together. Though I didn't understand why this scene would agitate me, I stayed at that balance point between the physical sensations and the images. I allowed them to be together. I allowed myself to not understand the connection.

Then my body led me to start breathing faster and something shifted. The energy I was feeling was still strong, perhaps even stronger, but suddenly it wasn't unsafe or uncomfortable. The fear left. Then I felt a lot of potential and creativity. Afterwards I realized the emotion I first recognized also contained this lighter feeling. I was learning to allow the feeling in my body, and that it was OK to be with those feelings, even when they're not resolved, clear, or entirely conscious.

Emotions are manifestations of unconscious intention. They are full of psychic and physical energy and information.

Emotions are manifestations of unconscious intention. They are full of psychic and physical energy and information. Your habit also may also be to shy away from the feelings that make you uncomfortable. With patience and sensitivity, you can not only be more present in these stronger feelings and energies, but you can enjoy them.

As you stay present with a charged feeling like that, it will begin to change in some way. It may become stronger. It may shift into another channel. When I awoke from my dream, the energy I was feeling had already shifted. The shift started in the emotional, imaginal state of the dream and flowed into my body. The physical response woke me up. Then when I was conscious and stayed with my charged feeling, the dream imagery came back to awareness, another channel shift. The next change I noticed was in my breathing. I was led into a mental insight. I began to feel more comfortable with the energy.

Whatever emotions or feelings you find challenging, you can learn to be present with them. Your body focus will help you focus. Any strong emotions, but especially feelings you avoid, can become guides to help you express your deeper unconscious.

Holding or allowing something that may be uncomfortable or edgy for you can be a very valuable experience. When you do an intuitive exercise, you may rush through the different steps in order to get to the feedback. Feedback is exciting, but also you may consider that the discomfort of not knowing may cause you to end the exercise quickly. With practice, you will be able to stay in that uncomfortable "not knowing" zone longer. In this transitory state, you begin to allow more time for subtler senses to develop. Often what is really meaningful will come through as you stay in the unknowing zone longer.

With practice, any discomfort you experience can be transformed into the satisfaction of a deeper self-exploration. When you allow some "unknown" sense into your awareness with you, not understanding what it is, you may even experience confusion. You can still stay open to the meaning it brings. Every new "unknown" arising in your consciousness can become a meditation, a slipping out of the mind into the dynamic present. On the surface there may seem be no connection to what you think should be happening, and little connection to your long-term dreams, hopes and goals. Deeper down though, everything that comes into your awareness relates to your entire becoming.

What is manifesting in your awareness now?
Can you attend to the qualities that are still on the edge of your awareness?
Relax into that wordless place.
Let it inform you...

Is it possible to imagine that what is happening is connected to what you want?

Being present now, you can make a choice that's more conscious about what to do next, or how to respond to what's happening. If you skip over an exercise here, then you may be operating out of a conclusion that what's happening here in this text won't get you what you want. That may be an accurate assessment. Is that what your deeper intentions tell you? On the other hand, a feeling of restlessness or a desire to skip something may inform you that something meaningful might be just at the edge of your awareness. What would it take to allow that soul-guided movement into your consciousness?

You can be present with yourself.
Do you want to skip something?
Are you in a hurry?
What is alive in you now?

Then check and see what you are experiencing?
Be present with that?

Can you take the time to respond to yourself?

By all means close the book and put it down if that's where your process takes you.

Unknown Others and Language

Sensing the arrival of a spontaneous "other" can be a magical experience, since it happens wholly outside of your normal sense of self. Part of the allure of meditation, intuition and altered states of consciousness is a hope that something other will come into our consciousness. The magical quality of being that comes with altered states is attractive and meaningful. I don't believe it is magical in the sense of being supernatural or illusory. Being present and conscious in an expanded state is natural and real. It is magical enough in the way it delights and captivates us.

What happens in that moment when something new spontaneously appears in your awareness? It's identical to what occurs when you immerse yourself in physical, sensory awareness. When you extend your awareness and move into your experiencing present, you open up, if only briefly, to an unknown. Your joy and the full engagement makes you feel totally alive. Then you are activated in some way by whatever you sense.

For example, if I pause now, I can lay my hand down on the desk where I'm writing. You can also do this while you read. Just rest one of your hands on something next to you. Then be receptive to what you sense. When I do this, I perceive an initial, familiar sense of hardness and some coolness. As I attend to these sensations, I notice the temperature quickly begins to change.

What is your perception?
Stay with your sensation for a few moments.

Then I become aware that the muscles in my hand have changed as well. There's a feeling of vibration I can just barely sense. I notice it more clearly as I attend to it. It seems related to the hardness of the table. At least that's the first mental association that comes up. The vibration runs up my arm into my body. I stay with it longer and I soon become aware of a pulsation, partly from my own pulse and partly from the hum of the computer resting on the table. The sensation continues even through the thoughts I have about it.

As I stay present with myself I become aware of a thicker sense difficult to describe. I first notice it in my stomach and on the back of my neck as I touch and then release the table with my hand. I've never been aware of this sense before and have no framework for it, no context. It feels a little like the feeling I have when I'm digesting food. The longer I stay with this sensing, the richer and more varied it becomes. It continues to change and become less familiar, and more interesting.

Can you stay with your sensing?
Perhaps you want to pause from reading for a few moments...

With each sense I allow and consider, I encounter different sensations and perceptions. The richness and complexity of the experience is totally new each time. Each element that is familiar builds my sensory awareness, like an alphabet forming a new language. But this is a language that is "in the moment" with new patterns of information. Jane Roberts offers one way to think about this kind of language:

> *Another partially deciphered Sumari script suggests that the word cordella rather than alphabet is used to break up usual conceptions connected with the word alphabet, while conveying an idea of symbols closely related, upon which alphabets are based. Seen in this way, there would be cordellas beneath the sensations of hearing, smelling, seeing, and so forth. The fragment further implies that the skin has its own alphabet.* [27]

If you stay with what you sense with your skin, or with other senses, in a non-logical way, you will begin to make sense of the language of that sense. You will become more familiar with the nuances, symbols, and energies of that language.

With practice, these non-cognitive forms of knowing become familiar. When I return to what I'm actually sensing, I always go into a flow of new experience that has depth and meaning. If I allow, I will begin to sense other things coming out of this flow, things that aren't directly related to the physical senses. From the sensations in my hand on the table for instance, my awareness shifted to a body sense that I've never experienced. From there, imagery may begin to appear or a smell or perhaps another body sensation. If I have an intuitive mental set, conscious or unconscious, the new information I perceive may carry intuitive meaning. When I stay receptive and present with the flow of sensation, I can perceive something wholly new and unknown. If I move into a willful state of mind, labeling or mentally deciding the meaning of what I'm sensing, then the flow of new information stops.

Sometimes I stop the flow. That can be a good thing. I can observe that too. I can observe how the activation of my mind also relates to my intentions. Often when I'm in a sensory flow, I find myself mentally processing something I've just sensed. For example, from the opening to that sense of vibration from my hand resting on the table, I found myself shifting back into a memory of another time I started to feel more physical sensations, and became self-conscious.

The shift from immersed sensing back to another, mental mode often happens spontaneously and unconsciously. I've learned I can also trust that shifting back. It is another level of intention becoming activated. It may be that I need to reorient myself. It may be that the next piece of the flow of my experience will come through the mental channel. It may be, as with my example, an opportunity to integrate some previous experience I've had. There is a constant balancing between the unconscious intentions and the conscious ones.

This shifting is similar to what happens during dream states. Sometimes when I'm having an interesting dream, I am awakened by something. If I was enjoying the dream, then I tend to resist waking. I was happy there; I want to go back into that dream. But there are other unconscious intentions bringing me out. When I remember to trust those other intentions, I can allow my self to let go, even when that takes me up into alert, waking consciousness.

Learning to trust your own flow starts here. You can allow an experience to lead you, however seemingly inconsequential or profound it is. You will come out of it when it is right for you. There can be a balanced equilibrium in the flow of your awareness leading you in and out of your deeper self. Allowing each experience to unfold in its own way will manifest meaning, understanding and significance that is relevant to you.

Can you imagine that if you need to leave these words and

text, to go into a different part of your consciousness, to activity or even to a quiet state, that there is an innate intelligence inside you guiding you?
Sense that guidance.
Enjoy it.
Invite that inner ally to lead you into the conscious experience of the deeper meaning of your life.

Have you been reading your way quickly through this book and doing all the exercises?

If so, I'd like you to pay attention to how your energy level influences your ability to focus. If you become tired, your body is speaking to you. Take a break.

You can also do these exercises at different times of the day, in different mental states, or in different physical places.

Chapter 15

Drawing Senses

You can experience another sensory shift, building on non-language ways to communicate inner experiences. Following this drawing practice, you will do another intuitive exercise. Read this exercise through first. Have some blank paper and a pen on hand.

> *Start touching objects that are around you with your non-writing hand.*
> *As you feel the object, its texture, temperature and hardness will become apparent.*
>
> *Enjoy those sensations.*
>
> *Then with your writing hand, draw the feeling you're experiencing.*
> *Don't try to draw the object or what you think it looks like, just draw the feeling.*
> *All you have to do is allow your non-writing hand to follow what you are feeling and allow the movement of your pen to follow that feeling.*
>
> *Experience that connection.*

Can you enjoy your drawing not making "sense"?

Remember, you are not drawing a picture, but a feeling.
It's not supposed to look like anything.

You can even close your eyes if you want to focus more on the feeling.

Then shift from one texture to another one, or perhaps to a temperature or a feeling of pressure.

Notice how your response changes when you shift your awareness to textures, hardness, or temperature.

Draw those changes as they occur in you.
Enjoy your drawing as long as you like.
Do it now.

Afterwards, describe your experience.
How did you feel?
Any body sensations, thoughts or emotions?

You can enjoy this exercise with each of your senses. Draw sounds, smells and emotions. After you've finished drawing each sense, you can go back and describe it. You will have a different perspective of the object you were sensing.

As you draw a sense, other information from the unconscious will flow into your awareness. Also, shifting into the flow of drawing puts you into a receptive frame of mind. From that place, you can enjoy another intuitive exercise.

Precognitive Newspaper

You can establish a very effective daily intuitive practice using a newspaper, an exercise in precognitive perception. You get a new target every single day and you get feedback. This picture will usually not be something you'll be able to guess. Even if you think you know what will be in the picture, you can work to perceive

Chapter 15   *175*

more detail. Your daily practice will refine your skills.

Here's an example from one of my daily practice sessions. First here's what I wrote and drew.

Figure 12

I put a square around the parts that I thought related to the photo. A circular shape with an up and down shape. Another image with a funnel shape and the words, "Funnel up, Red or Red flowing," and tight curly shapes and the words, "How = curly shapes." I also put a square around the words, "Inside a building (bldg), roller = what, fun = why."

Here's the photo that was on that day's newspaper:

Figure 13

It shows some women holding balloons in a small room as part of a celebration. The balloons are red. They are indoors, in a small room. You can see the curly shapes of the string used to tie the balloons and the strings and balloons form a "V" shape.

You can do this exercise at different times of day. Take a break and do it now. Start with different senses. Try meditating or drawing first. Find a flow that works for you.

Follow the format with the homework form on pages 142-144. Do a body focus first and center yourself. Then when you get to step #4, your intent will be, "What will be the largest picture on the cover of tomorrow's newspaper?" Then relax and allow what comes into your awareness. If you wish you can imagine yourself looking at the paper, in the position you will be in when you get it. Then let your perceptions come.

When you've written down, described and drawn everything, then set your work aside and wait until you get your feedback. When you get your feedback, fully sense the largest picture and describe it. Then you will be able connect your intuitive awareness to the feedback.

Peak Experiences

Sometimes when we enter into a new experience a deep part of us says "Yes." We are ready for it and we really do let go. Even a simple exercise like drawing a texture can open a door within us and become deeply profound. It may seem as though the activity we were engaged in caused the experience. But these peak experiences are also made possible by unconscious forces within us. The external stimulus may simply provide the catalyst to trigger our own internal readiness.

I believe we're "hard wired" for deeper, immersed or peak experiences. They are the expression of our deeply sensual nature. Though euphoric and even blissful, these kind of experiences can also be very unsettling. As in the immersed perception figure on page 127, a sudden opening can suddenly transform your sense of self or your reality. You may come through a profound, immersed experience changed.

Returning from any kind of immersed or profound experience can be confusing. Your mind may kick in and try to reorient you to where you were before. You may start telling yourself your experience wasn't real or that you were just hallucinating. You may also know deeply that it was real and be saddened that you are no longer experiencing that level of meaning or bliss.

> **Effectively integrating altered state experiences has to do with letting go of the feelings or thoughts we are having.**

Having familiarity with your changing mental states can be very helpful, making profound states easier to integrate. Effectively integrating altered state experiences has to do with letting go of the feelings or thoughts we are having. Feelings of expansion, joy, or spaciousness may be very profound and attractive, but they can still be allowed to pass. Waking from that incredible dream, coming down from a real high, or coming back into your normal way of being is still part of the natural flow of your awareness. Our most familiar states of consciousness help to ground us and allow us to integrate our most profound experiences.

Living the Process

Consciousness in flow ceases to be up or down, positive or negative. Even ideas of bliss or love are abstractions from our actual experience, ways that we frame them with our conscious mind. In a self-awareness practice, we learn to identify ourselves as a flow and a process more than as a content of experience.

If you're about to board a plane, and you experience a feeling of dread, you can attend to it. You can be with that feeling even if it's a shift from what you thought you were supposed to be feeling. You may have an image of a crash and experience other powerful, uncomfortable emotions. You can be aware, right in that moment, and decide what you need to do.

In that moment, it doesn't matter if there actually will be a plane crash or not. You may be perceiving an accurate precognition or it may be a personal fear. Regardless, you can move forward within inner and outer congruence. In the next moment it may feel right to sit down and not board the plane. You drop into yourself and your present senses guide you. As time passes, it may be that the plane is delayed. Then later it may be OK to board the plane. It may be that the feeling passes and it becomes OK to continue with the flight. Being present with yourself, you can flow through the whole experience with consciousness, curiosity and focus.

Fear can be a learned response to large amounts of energy or unknown energies. Being present with that energy may transform it into your personal power. If you imagine you're going to die if you get on that plane, you can easily get caught up in fear, doubt or skepticism. Yet, your deepest sense of self is outside of fear, joy, longing or any conscious limitation. When you are present with your self, the response that arises in you in that moment may be simply to breathe or to sit down. Then something else will arise in the next moment of your process. You may sense a need to speak or to become more alert. Perhaps your body will need to move.

It doesn't matter how intense the energy you are experiencing is. You can be aware of it, attend to it, and respond to it with presence and consciousness. It does take practice to flow consciously through strong energies. Your ability begins now as you explore unknown feelings and sensations.

In quiet moments like this...
All you have to do is attend.
You are learning to handle the flow of your life in all its varied expressions.
You are building the practice that guides you in moments that are more active, more charged with energy and emotion.

Learning to trust the flow of your awareness leads to self-confidence and self-protection. All of your different levels of intention manifest in the present in your mind/body. A need or intention for self-protection will manifest in you in a recognizable way. In the case of the plane, if there were a real danger, an unconscious part of you would have sensed it. Your bad feeling or clear image would have been a signal your conscious mind recognized.

As you explore inner awareness and consciousness, it's very easy to dissociate from the physical. I believe transformations of consciousness include the whole being—mind, body, heart, and spirit. Your physical body will drop away at some point, but right now it is a part of who you are. Taking time to attend to your body will help you balance and integrate what you learn through consciousness explorations. Every time you proceed with an exercise take a moment and tune into your body. Become aware of what your body is telling you. Respond to what it tells you. Honor your body as a healthy part of your system of balances.

Perhaps you could breathe again, more deeply, into your body, connecting these thoughts to your physical being, and responding with movement if necessary.

Chapter 16

Beliefs and Fears

There are many cultural beliefs about intuition and psychic abilities. I asked you fill out the belief questionnaire earlier to start making your beliefs conscious. As with the other writing exercises in this book, writing down your beliefs brings them out of the realm of the unconscious.

Take a moment now and think again about what, if any, fears you may have about intuition or psychic abilities.
Do you have any other fears about psychic abilities that you didn't write down?
If so, you can add to your list.

People commonly fear loss of control, an inability to turn intuition off or being overpowered by it, loss of sense of self, fear that these abilities are a trap and a detour from true spiritual progress, an invitation to become psychically possessed by malevolent entities.

These fears are directly related to beliefs about what intuition and psi powers are all about. For example, you might believe intuition is mediated by a higher power. What happens if you go against the wishes of that power? Are there consequences?

You may believe there is a moral basis to your use of intuition. Are there times when it is wrong to use intuition? What happens if you break the rules? Do you lose your abilities?

In my mind these are all legitimate concerns, if they are concerns for you and you believe in them. The closer these beliefs are to your core sense of self, the more they influence your behavior, and the more threatening it will feel to you to challenge or shift these beliefs.

You can respect your beliefs and respond accordingly. You can alter any exercise you do in this book to suit your comfort level. For example, did it feel wrong for you to ask questions about a friend, without getting permission first? If so, then ask permission of your higher power, spirit, or your friend before you proceed.

> When strong emotions arise you have a great opportunity to learn about yourself.

As a part of your awareness practice, you also have an opportunity to become aware of your beliefs and test how valuable they are for you. If one of the exercises in this book or some of the ideas feel wrong to you, take a moment and ask yourself why. Explore why you feel this way.

When strong emotions arise, you have a great opportunity to learn about yourself. I'll use fear as an example, but the learning opportunity applies to any strong emotion, positive or negative.

You can perceive fear when it rises just like any other sensation. Doing the body focus will help you make your fear more conscious. Feeling the fear in your body brings you into the experience of the fear and out of your interpretation of it. It will then flow and change just like any other sensation. The flow will bring in insights, memories and connections to other times you felt similar feelings. The more you can stay with the feeling of fear, the more you will be able to understand what beliefs are connected to it. You will be able to respond to your fear with your whole being. Also, having an intention to understand your fear will help bring out the information you need to know.

If your personal feelings aren't allowed, perceived and released, they will effectively stop all intuitive perception. Andreas Mavromatis talks about this stoppage as it occurs in the hypnagogic state:

> *Sometimes, while in this relaxed state, a fearful idea or image may rise into consciousness resulting in a switch to focal attention and active mode, thus terminating the state. ...it would explain why hypnagogia cannot be maintained in the presence of fear or anxiety.*[22]

The same is true for intuition. When you become personally afraid of something, intuition shuts down. In order to proceed, you have to be able to move out of the fear or know how to manage the energy of it consciously and safely. Psychics who do forensic work learn how. They are constantly dealing with dangerous or violent content, but they know how to stay stable and safe. They understand their feelings and know how to manage them in a healthy way.

Charles Tart [31] suggests a process for dealing with strong fears associated with developing psi abilities. The subject starts with acknowledgement of the feelings, develops coping skills or ways of responding to these emotions, accepts responsibility and in the end grows and evolves.

The body focus starts your process by helping you acknowledge the emotions and fears you may be experiencing. By practicing the body focus, you become familiar with every day feelings and will then be more able to stay present with stronger fears when they arise.

Do you know what your physiological response is to fear?

Do you know what happens to your thinking?

What happens when you sit with these feelings in your body?

This kind of basic awareness helps you recognize the feeling of fear. You will be more conscious before you fall into your automatic response. You then have an opportunity not only to manage your fear, but also to learn what the fear is trying to communicate. Fear is a felt experience first and foremost, one that you can attend to. If there is meaning, power, or energy behind the fear, it will manifest as you stay with it. Fear can give you feedback as valuableas the feedback from any positive emotion. You will learn that naming and experiencing sensations releases them, and you will be able to flow through fear in the same way.

Once you learn to be more balanced with fear or other uncomfortable feelings, you can respond with genuine appropriateness. Self-respect, nurturing and personal protection will come into play and help you cope with your feelings. You will do what you need to do to feel safe. You will learn how to respond to the symptoms of fear and other strong emotions in a healthy way. You will take care of yourself.

> The more you develop your sense of self, the more you can integrate experiences that come from other states of consciousness.

Perhaps you will remember to breathe or go for a walk and get into your body. You may also remind yourself that you're OK and that you are safe. When you are conscious of a fear, know what it is, and know where it takes you, then you have choices. Strong emotions and energies can be allowed to become part of your whole being. You can respect your fear, learn to live with it and act congruently with all the parts of you.

Fear serves a valuable purpose. It alerts us to danger or to threats. Knowing what the danger is allows us to move through the feelings of fear. A psychic on a crime scene uses her emotional response to hone in on her goal, for example, the location of the crime. Ghost hunters do the same thing.

When the sense of fear arises, it alerts them to other changes occurring in their environment. The first indication of fear becomes a signal to be aware. If fear ever becomes too uncomfortable, then steps are taken for personal safety. For average people, fear is often one of the first signs that we are approaching something important.

It may be a sign of our new edge, a place where we're growing, need to go, and want to go. Fear becomes our ally and a guide.

The next step to integrate fear, or any strong emotion, is accepting responsibility. It is definitely possible to respond in aggressive or manipulative ways with information we've received intuitively. As you learn and experience what is possible with intuition, you might fear misuse. You can take responsibility for yourself and the abilities you have. The professional psychics that I know have learned to turn off their abilities except for when they are specifically requested. They respect other individuals and themselves. They would burn out if they had intuitive channels open all the time.

Lastly, developing intuition will become your process of personal growth. The more you develop your sense of self, the more you can integrate experiences that come from other states of consciousness. Strong emotions are also altered states. Your ability to embody those emotions will make you more congruent. Your ego-self will be grounded in your experiencing body. The more work you do on yourself, the stronger foundation you'll have for your own consciousness exploration. You will grow and mature through the course of self-exploration and expansion.

Are you in your body now?

Having the flexibility to shift between the physical, emotional, mental and spiritual parts of your awareness lets you express your whole being. Strong emotions often have a lot of energy associated with them. That energy will often release with physical movement. Where insight or intuition may be the expression of energy in the mental realm, movement is the expression of energy in the body. Your physical movement can be anything that feels right.

Even now as you're reading, is your body responding in some way?
Pay attention to its movement.
Allow it to lead you into the next moment.

Integrating the Body

In the classes I've taught, I've seen many students who seemed to be quite disconnected from their bodies. For intuitive seekers, this may be partly because of the intensity of focus on non-physical experience. Also, we live in a culture that trains us very effectively to narrow focus on our goals and our intentions. We use the same narrow focus to study spirit and consciousness. When held too long, this narrow focus becomes stressful. We dissociate from other parts of ourselves and other ways of being. The healthy integration that can happen with the spontaneous movement of our energy can be totally cut off when we're very focused on a task. Shifting from that objective focus and coming back into the body opens up our spontaneous energy focus.

If you tend to disconnect with your physical side, start activating it again. Take up a practice that gets you into your body. I hope you even get to the point where you can put down this book and connect with yourself.

Do you feel the need to integrate your physical body?

The more balanced you are with your physical self, the more that strength and solidity stays with you in your mental space. Being integrated in mind and body doesn't need to be externally active. In an intuitive exercise, the openness of a quiet body can allow very subtle sensations to become conscious. Having a healthy, integrated physical awareness increases intuitive sensitivity. Your body becomes a solid base for your psychic explorations.

> *Take a deep breath and remember a time in your life when you felt totally grounded, connected to all the parts of yourself, comfortable and alive.*
>
> *(No memories? Then imagine some.)*
>
> *Breathe into that memory for a few moments.*
> *Activate your senses.*

*Your remembering now connects you to resources and
strengths that you always carry with you.
You can activate that sense and feeling now.*

*Notice if there is one sense you particularly enjoy.
If so, then consider how that sense may be supporting and
balancing the other parts of you.
Let it guide you into a grounded connection, inside.*

*Is there a movement that arises from within this feeling?
Allow that as well.
Enjoy this sensory connection as long as you like.*

Emotions become too strong or fearful when they are locked up in some way, when they're not allowed to move in the body. One way to release them and return to a feeling of safety is by remembering an experience where you felt 'on' and in your body. You can remember it, go with it in your imagination, and move into your body. To be effective, your imagining must be allowed to move into your body. If you can, do the movement that you imagine. Go for a walk, stretch, or exercise. Love the feeling of being in your physical body.

Envisioning in the Body

For example, I do have a wonderful, relaxing memory of being on vacation at a tropical beach. I can think of being there and remember an image of myself relaxed, lying in a hammock. But if I just think it, I stay completely in my mind with this memory. If that happens, I won't re-experience the positive feelings I had when I was there.

To get to the feelings, I allow myself to go deeper and "get into" my senses. I remember the texture of the hammock and the feel of the air against my body. Then the smell of the ocean, the sunscreen, and even the faint smell of barbecue drifting down the beach comes back to me. I allow myself to go into these feelings and my body starts to respond. I actually start to feel those sensations. Without even realizing it consciously, I let go of the tension in my shoulders and neck. My body memory returns. Then the emotional energy I was feeling releases and begins moving again.

Here are some suggestions to help you envision:

> *Imagine that your deepest spiritual center, that which connects you with God or your higher power, is actually a presence that surrounds you right now.*
> *You can sense this presence as a cocoon of beautiful light completely surrounding your body. It extends all the way around you, and even into your body, acting as a protective force and a shield.*
> *With each breath that flows through you, that energy field grows larger, stronger and clearer.*
> *You can sense the energy of it on your skin, tingling with energy.*
> *You can feel it inside you, with a gentle warmth.*
> *As your mind and body become quieter and relax into this protective sense, you begin to hear this field around you as well.*
> *You hear its presence and feel the vibrations of the sound in your body.*

> *Enjoy all that safety and comfort as deeply as you like.*

> *How does this feel?*

> *Can you feel the physical sense of the light?*
> *Is there a sound or a smell that goes with it?*

> *The more senses you activate, the more you activate your mind and body.*
> *Feel the movements of the air in and out of your body, breathing in the color and sound.*
> *Attend to your heart.*
> *Bring its rhythm into the flow of your awareness.*

> *Let your imagining evolve.*

You can be guided by unconscious forces.
As you imagine yourself in a positive way, your body will respond.
You can trust your experience to unfold as is right for you.

Do it now.
Then describe your experience.

When you create a safe and comfortable feeling, you can integrate difficult emotions from a place of greater stability and safety. Then with calmness and connection, you can face your fears or anxieties.

The meaning of your feelings will come from the experience of them, not from what your mind decides they are. When you're feeling a familiar emotion, it's easy to assume you know what it means and to give it a label. But this only serves to separate you from it and stops the flow of information. That feeling though, when allowed and experienced, may provide wholly new meaning that is relevant to you present awareness. Your mind will come in with understanding and insight.

Mind, body and spirit can be balanced and integrated. You can experience the non-verbal, non-conscious insights that come from your body, heart, spirit or unconscious. You can allow the natural transitions to other ways of knowing. One may already be happening even while you're reading...

Let go for a moment and shift gears.
Stand up, stretch, do whatever you need to do.
What guidance is the rest of your being bringing you now?

Chapter 17

Suggestion

When we're absorbed or fascinated by something, our conscious mind becomes quiet. Then, in this receptive state there is less resistance to suggestions that resonate within us. Affirmations and suggestions are another way to deepen the connections between your conscious and your subconscious. Your affirmations and suggestions allow other parts of yourself that are manifesting to become more real. It is a powerful way we learn. This deep suggestibility is one of the primary therapeutic functions of hypnosis. Your unconscious mind will respond, regardless o the difficulties your conscious mind perceives. Bernard Baars clarifies this in <u>The Theater of Consciousness</u>:

> *...suggestion is merely the ordinary functioning of consciousness without the added mental operation of self-doubt. The reason why in "hypnosis" we can extend an arm rigidly with unsuspected strength is that we do not entertain doubts about our ability to do it. Presumably in absorbed states there is simply no room for self-doubt, or for any other metacognitive, self-conscious thoughts.* [2]

In the absence of doubt, we accomplish whatever we clearly

intend with high efficiency. Suggestions have the most effect when they are congruent with our deep intent. We let go into resonance. In my hypnotherapy practice, I've seen how a few well-placed suggestions, ones that truly resonate with a person's deeper sense of self, can have tremendous, lasting influence. The right words come from me when I am "in tune" and reflecting back what a client communicates to me.

You can develop a practice to give yourself meaningful suggestions. You can connect them to significant experiences, feelings or emotions and they'll have more positive effect. Would you like to experience this world in a joyful, loving and creative way? Then start by imagining it. You can put yourself into your image.

> *Remember a place or a time when you felt joyful, loving and creative.*
> *Take some breaths and remember the sensations and feelings you experienced.*
> *Allow those memories to come into your body.*
>
> *When you feel it, say to yourself,*
>
> *I am feeling joyful, loving and creative.*
> *This world is a joyful, loving and creative place.*

When you think that thought as you're feeling it, you validate what is happening. If it's congruent with your deeper intentions, you open the door for more of these feelings and insights. These affirmations are easier to accept when you're really feeling them. They still work when you've forgotten or lost touch with what you know in your deeper self.

When you're in a frustrated or disconnected state of mind and you give yourself a suggestion, you may have an internal critic that replies, "Get real. Life just isn't that way." or "Maybe for some people, but not for me." You may not believe the words you're thinking. Use these suggestions to respond to that inner critic:

> *Pay attention to the thoughts in your mind.*

What are the corresponding feelings in your body?

You might ask yourself whose voice you are hearing?
Where did it come from?
Do you believe what it says?

Be with the experience and observe it.
You could even describe it or draw the feelings.

Remember, a strong belief, when you hear it speaking, seems like the only reality, but it is still changeable. Even if you do have a particularly harsh internal critic, your unconscious will still respond to the suggestions that resonate within you. Just as you've learned to do things to nurture your physical body, you can begin to nurture your mind. You can start commenting on things you do that reaffirm your clear intent. Say you're about to undertake a project and you have this critical thought,

"I can't do that."

Then you think about it for a moment and realize the thought is just one of your old critic's comments. So you think to yourself,

"Maybe I just think I can't do that."

You then think more about what you're doing and recognize it may be challenging, but still is very do-able. So you say to yourself,

"Yes I can do this."
And after more thought you add, "I am creative, loving, aware
*   and filled with joy."*

The last phrase comes out of your feelings in that moment because you're happy, you've already shifted your thinking. Being present with yourself and paying attention to your process, you begin to change. But you can go even further. Right then, you can compliment yourself. You could say,

> *"Well done (your name). That was good. I can change my thoughts. I am on the right track! I can enjoy my own abilities and resources even more now."*

With suggestions, you can speak to yourself in ways that are positive and congruent to your deepest sense of who you are. You can do more than not be critical; you can be complimentary. Rather than allow an inner critic to run loose inside your psyche, you can modify your thinking. You can choose thoughts that support you, and that support your strengths.

> *Which voice do you want speaking to you?*
> *Does it have a name?*
> *Is it speaking now?*
> *Listen.*

Of course, there are times when you need caution and skepticism. But that skeptical part doesn't have to lead you through all of the rest of your life experiences. If you feel you're going too fast, then let the cautious part speak. Welcome its guidance. Any time your heart opens and you feel your spirit move, you can compliment and validate yourself. A personal comment to yourself at the right time will allow new possibilities to grow and flourish.

If your life is an education, a path of self-discovery and a building of awareness, then you may want to think seriously about who you want to guide you. Do you want to follow the part of you that can see the big picture, that knows your strengths and weaknesses, and has the wisdom to guide you well?

> *What part of you would provide that guidance?*
> *Can you sense it now?*

> *Tune into that part. Feel its presence inside of you.*
> *Take a moment and invite that part to speak.*
> *Allow it to guide you.*

Listen to this voice as it sets you on the path of abundant living. You can tailor some autosuggestions to affirm what you are. It doesn't matter which form that guide takes. It must fit you and feel right. That is the most important thing.

Giving yourself suggestions may seem awkward at first. That's OK. Just start, try them on, and see how they work. See how they feel. Be present with your inner responses as well. You are building a new way of being. Be patient and allow this part of you to grow.

What would you say to yourself now to reinforce what you are learning?
Can you speak from the part you want to lead you?

Personal Suggestions

Here's an exercise to help you use positive suggestions. You can do this one as you read. First of all make yourself comfortable.

Be aware of what you're feeling in your body and mind.
Describe a bit of what's alive in you.
Do your feelings have any meaning for you?
Is there anything you need to respond to?

Become aware of your breathing.
Take several deep breaths in and out.
Let the awareness of your breath bring you back into you body.
Give yourself time.
Stay with yourself and your breathing for a few moments and allow your balance and inner connection to return.

Imagine a place you like to go, a place that makes you feel good, a place that gives you positive feelings.
Revivify the memories of that place.
Engage your senses with these memories and feelings.
As you enjoy them, let them become stronger.
Take some time with each one of your senses.
Enjoy what you experience.

All of your senses connect you to a deeper part of your own being.

Take your time.
Let your felt sense stay with you as you continue reading.

Consider and respond to the following questions.

1 - If you could have anything you wanted right now to aid you on your path to total self awareness, what would it be?

Think about it.
Be honest with yourself.
Be detailed.

Here are some examples: (If you don't want examples, then skip this part after each question.)

I would like a better job, a job where I enjoy myself, where I'm learning.
I would like to lose weight. I would like to feel lighter, slimmer and more healthy.
I would like to be healthy, in mind, body, spirit.
I would like to know my purpose in life.
I would like to have a loving partner, a soul mate.
I would like to live my life with a person connected in this way.
I would like more close friends and honesty.

Describe what you would like now.

2 - Ask yourself what are you already doing to make your wishes happen?

Example: I'm reading books that inspire me. I'm taking a class. I eat good food. I exercise.

Write down everything you are doing, even if it seems trivial or insignificant.

3 - Then consider. What else you could do right now to make your intentions happen?
Example: I could exercise more regularly. I could join a group.

Write down what you could do.

4 - If you came up with things you could do, then pay attention to them. You may need to take some physical action to get what you want. It may not be easy to actually do something about it, but it's very important to put your deeper wants into action.

5 - Now activate your imagination. Imagine you have what you want. Imagine that you have reached that goal. You may even imagine you are forward in time if you like. Imagine having all of it. What would you be doing, thinking, or feeling then? Be specific.

Example: If I had that job, all the pressure I feel now would be gone. My body would feel better. I'd be sleeping better. I'd be happy to get up in the morning, I'd feel excited to go to work. I'd feel needed, valued and creative.

Imagine that now.
How would you know it?
How would you feel?
What else would you be experiencing?

Be specific.
Elaborate on those thoughts and feelings.

6 - Now continue to imagine that you are doing those things and feeling these new ways. Go through each action you are thinking and feeling. As you imagine, I want you to be aware how you feel. Comment on how you feel in the present. Use the present tense and say "I am."
Example: I am so happy and confident. I can take on the

world. I'm easy with myself, likable and attractive. My entire body feels healthy and full of energy.

> *Become aware how these activities and changes make you feel.*
> *As you are aware of your feelings, write them down.*
> *And of course, enjoy those feelings.*

7 - Now imagine you could be observing yourself doing these things and feeling that way. Imagine that person you're observing was a child of yours, or a person very dear to you, a person you love. What would you tell her to encourage her, to give her support? What would you tell her to affirm her progress? Say these words to her and write down every positive thing you say. Is there any positive part you see in her that she isn't aware of? Compliment her on that. Bring it to her attention.

Example: You are so confident. You move gracefully and smoothly and with strength. You do such good work. You are inspired and guided. You just radiate confidence. You are so loving and considerate. You are stronger than you think.

> *What would you tell her to encourage them, to give her support? What would you tell her to affirm what she is already doing? What would you say to her that would really affirm and support her in a positive healing way?*

8 - As you say these things, notice how it feels to hear those words.

> *How would it feel to hear those comments spoken to you?*
> *Take a few moments, to be aware of what you're experiencing.*
> *Enjoy yourself.*
> *Breathe.*

> *Then describe your thoughts and feelings.*
What you wrote for steps seven and eight can be used as sug-

gestions to compliment yourself. They are for you. They speak to something important that you want to manifest in your life.

They may also seem too good to be true and a little hard to accept. There may be an internal critic or a younger part of you that feels awkward. If so, love that part of you and welcome the awkwardness. Then remember how you arrived at those words. They evolved from feeling what you want. All of those thoughts and images are important to you. You do deserve all of that and more. Those words are designed by you and for you to help you become all you want to be. You can accept those statements right down to the core of your being. You can allow yourself to receive those words with an open heart and mind.

You can talk to yourself using phrases like that every time you do something that furthers your progress. How are you feeling now having gone through that exercise? Do you enjoy what you are feeling? Then,

> *Repeat those supporting and guiding words to yourself right now.*
> *Connect them to your feelings.*
> *Enjoy how it feels to hear those words.*
>
> *You may also want to start saying things like that to other people.*
> *Since you know how good it feels, you can give that gift freely.*

This is one way to come up with positive suggestions to give yourself. Circle the phrases from that exercise you would like to hear more often. Write them down somewhere so you can see them. Those are your suggestions. Read them often until they come spontaneously. Then every time you do anything that furthers you in any way, compliment yourself. Validate what you are doing. Speak those phrases from your heart to your heart. You can also repeat this exercise and elaborate on what you would say. The more honestly you tune into your feelings, the better you will feel when you hear those words spoken to you.

You can allow yourself to feel that good as often as you like.

How about when you brush your teeth? Is that is beneficial for you, then say so. Recognize it. "Ahhhh.... that feels food. I am taking care of myself." This is how autosuggestions empower you. You can rescript how you think and feel and bring the value of this positive thought into every aspect of your life.

So right now, notice how you're feeling.
Has this exercise shifted your awareness in some way?
Look around the room where you are now. Tune in to what you are sensing.
Staying aware of your surroundings, read those suggestions to yourself one more time and enjoy the words.
Enjoy the feelings because they're true right now.
Feel yourself resonating with your thoughts and feelings.
What you are experiencing now is connected to the feeling and intent of your suggestions.
Let that new sense carry you into new perception and awareness.

As you practice, you will also become aware of other suggestions you give yourself. We all have inner commentary streaming through our minds. You can be more conscious of these thoughts. Do they serve you now? If not, you can shift them. You can let go of them, and you can love yourself in the process.

There is power in positive thought. An effective autosuggestion speaks to both parts of yourself, where you are now, and where you're going. Your conscious thoughts connect with your deeper purpose and you are in clear intent. Full awareness in the present moves you forward with more clarity towards your goals. The future part of yourself responds. The goals that you're striving for may not be physically manifest at the moment, but they are within your consciousness.

Chapter 18

Levity and Affirmation

The physical world and its forces are an integral part of lives. For example, you live within the pull of gravity every moment of your life. Right now, if you relax into it you can feel the embrace of gravity through the chair you're sitting in. You can sink down into the embrace of the earth. You live within it and it is a safe, familiar force. Gravity also keeps your spirits anchored to this physical realm. This force has a mirror side that is also essential. Victor Schauberger [11], the visionary Austrian forester and engineer, proposed that there is an equal but opposite force present - levity. Levity is always present as a counterpart to gravity. They are two sides of the same force.

What causes a tree to grow straight up 100 feet above ground? What forces allow a flea to want to jump 100 times its body length through space? What is it that causes us to rise up out of bed every morning against the pull of gravity? This life energy carries you elegantly, naturally and with grace right through and beyond the perceived constraints of physical reality. Nurturing and attending to deeper parts of yourself opens up your own levity, your spirit, a rising up of your consciousness and life force.

Invite your inner ally to lift you up.

Remind yourself that as you resonate with these words and ideas, you are activating your life force. New insights are forming and, along with them, new intentions.

Imagine how what are experiencing now is in some way already manifesting your deepest self.
Follow that.

Willis Harman, past director of the Institute of Noetic Sciences, made an affirmation for himself at the age of sixty:

"I have only one desire, and that is to know the deepest part of myself and to follow that." [17]

He would take five minutes every day, say this to himself, and then vividly imagine it being true. He felt that this simple intentional practice changed his life. His intention and the effort of actively imagining how to live his life connected to his deepest self is what made the affirmation effective for him. Thought, intention, and feeling all combine in the present and stir much larger forces within us. Your intent moves closer to your heart, resonating with your deep self as you practice sensing it and responding to it.

You can invite your spiritual presence into the present body of your experience.
Can you imagine that now?

To manifest change, you start by resonating with it—living it, breathing it and becoming it. By making it real, you stop wishing for it or seeking something outside of yourself. There's a part of you outside of time already connected to what you desire. Your affinities and your fascinations lead you toward future events, not by seeking the future, but by responding in the "now" to the present sense of enlivened feelings and to the energy they bring. The excitement we feel resonates with a part of ourselves that is outside of time.

Meeting my wife was this way for me. As we started dating, we quickly moved into a depth and connection that surpassed the limited time we had spent together. I believe these feelings were precognitive, non-timebound memories. I felt that the depth of our connection, which was outside of time, guided our present.

We both struggled to understand these forces consciously as we fell in love. We both shifted in and out of not trusting, then relaxing and trusting again, coming in and out of our minds in the process. When I shifted from the logic of my mind into my heart, the unfolding of that relationship became easier to follow and to trust. When we attend to those subtle future nudges as we experience them, we move into an elegance and flow that can be delightful.

If we don't attend to these soul movements, they may still manifest in time, but we may struggle more within ourselves to accept or allow what is happening.

> *Have there been moments in your life when it felt as though your future was opening?*
> *Have there been times when you felt a synchronicity with outside events?*
> *Remember the felt sense of those moments.*
> *You can invite that kind of flow and connection.*
>
> *Now become aware of your body again. Are there physical needs asking for attention? If so, then pay attention.*

Intuitive Target

With your book open in front of you, read and shift into receptive awareness. Read each suggestion in italics and take as much time as you need.

> *Remember what it feels like to shift to a passive, receptive frame of mind.*
> *Allow your body to remember your felt sense of shifting.*
>
> *Become aware of what you are sensing.*
> *Check in briefly with your senses.*
> *Focus on one at a time,*

Then allow each one to fade away.

Breathe for a minute or two...
Become more entranced with your present experience.

There is another intuitive target you can perceive.
You can move your intention towards it.
Be aware of what you sense and respond.
Allow your body to move if it needs to.

Ask questions and wait for responses.
Notice any changes you experience.
Describe what you experience.
Write down or draw what you perceive.

Take your time.
Enjoy yourself.
Do it now.

When you are done, you can allow your awareness to shift back to your normal orientation. Are you ready for feedback? The target of this exercise is what is imaged on the cover of the current issue of National Geographic Magazine. You can find it in your library, or see the cover image online at: http://ngm.nationalgeographic.com/

As always, when you view the image, pay attention to how it resonates with you. Engage your senses with your feedback. Sketch it and describe it with all your senses. Then take a moment and see what connections there are between the target and your intuitive perceptions.

Describe what you learned from this exercise.

The ritual you use to access intuition doesn't have to become a rule. Once you've learned how to experience a state of awareness, you can move directly into that state bypassing the external tools required. If you like what you experience when you are guided into a relaxation process, then bring it to mind and remember the experience. Your body memory will guide you into the sensations you experienced with the guided experience.

Your experiences may appear to be caused by something external - a book, an exercise, or a person - but you are still their creator. You might try a relaxation tape and experience a profound letting go. Your engagement with the tape manifests a profound part of yourself. You created it with your intention and brought it into your life through the tape. That feeling was already inside you waiting to manifest.

Now, once you've had the conscious experience of that deep relaxation and letting go, it remains yours. You can remember and experience a new sense of it any time you want. Consciously, you may decide that your experience was caused by the tape. Yet the tape was only a trigger to release your own capacities. Each time you go directly to your own resources, you embody more of the power behind the experience.

The external world is valuable and important. What you experience externally becomes part of you and you expand and grow. There is an exchange of energy and information as you engage in new experiences, as you become present to each sensation and experience you encounter. In the flow of being present, all of your experience, inner and outer, is part of your deeper spirit becoming.

Entangled Thinking

In Shamanic thinking, the world of our external experience is related to our personal consciousness. A healer traveling to visit her patient will acknowledge that what she perceives in the natural world will relate to the work she is about. An animal passing by or a change in the weather will be connected in some way with what is alive in her patient. Being conscious of those perceptions, she arrives with more information about the wholeness of the world as it relates to her patient. The healing she is about to do is not a discrete part of her life. It is intimately woven into the whole of her being.

Even the unconscious messages that arise in your body/mind are part of your connection to the larger field of consciousness.

When you allow the connection with subconscious and higher consciousness aspects of your self, your conscious self can become more "in touch" or informed. Even internal imagery, fantasies, or daydreams may take on an oracular quality, as in a night time dream. They may be revealing to you what you need to know about something happening in your life, your relationships or your body.

Every arrival that comes from outside conscious awareness has the potential to be a message from our higher selves.

How is your external world or your dreaming world already speaking to you?
What aspect of your deeper self is already being revealed in the outer world?
How can you open more to that greater connection?

Memories arise out of your now and thus carry an awareness that is different that what you had during the original experience.

Even when your intention moves towards the past it is not time bound. Memories arise out of your "now" and thus carry an awareness that is different from what you had during the original experience. If you remember something and allow that resonance to stay with you as you engage in the present, you move into new, "present moment" experience. You move forward from the remembering into the future unfolding of your self.

The same out-of-time awareness is part of any intention you have. It comes from what you have already experienced and moves you forward. What about having an intention to become intuitive, for example? You may have had an intuitive experience or even heard about intuition from someone else. Though your concept of intuition is based on memory—from reading, experience, of hearing stories—you can be fully present with the intention unfolding in the "now," becoming something new in this moment. When your intentions are dissociated from your experiencing body, it's easy to become trapped in your ideas. At some point you have to let go of the idea and "remember" what is happening in the present.

How is the beauty of your being manifesting in this moment? Look around you...

Figure 14

Spirit Connections

For many people, learning intuition is part of their spiritual awakening or exploration. If you believe you are on a spiritual path, your idea or your mental construct of that path, can keep you from experiencing what is happening. Whose path is it? Who told you what you were doing was spiritual? You may be trying to live someone else's notions of a path. To become present to your own path may take letting go of all your "ideas" about it. Your intention towards spirit will manifest in your awareness, as long as your idea and intent is balanced with your experiencing body. Your personal meaning of "spiritual" will arise inside your experiencing body.

Arising out of experience, your mind will fill in a framework of understanding. Your sense of self in the present is primary to the knowledge you attain. One teacher whose perspective guided me on my path was the Indian saint, Ramana Maharshi [21]. He said to know spirit, a seeker needed first and foremost to know himself. He would commonly answer a seeker's question with the question, "Who wants to know?" Then he would continue with,

> *"Find out who wants to know and you will understand all your questions."* [42]

He suggested that everything else a person needed would unfold out of that knowing. If you were to follow a path to enlightenment all you had to do is to ask the question, "Who am I?" Everything your mind came up with as an answer would be something you could objectify. Thus it would be separate from you and "not I." This questioning would point you closer to knowing your self.

This line of inquiry is very similar to the path of sensory awareness. You start with now, with what is known and is present in the now. Then from within your experience you unfold naturally in the present. That unfolding is your own authentic movement and will be meaningful to you. The more you reside within your own dynamic becoming, the more natural and graceful your path becomes.

Attend to the richness and subtlety of your whole being—your body, your being, your heart, even your dreaming state—and you find a way to open to this guidance. You are practicing intuition.

> *What is arising within you at this moment?*
> *What question is your spirit asking you?*
> *How flexible can you be in your response?*

As you attend to yourself, you may perceive many different levels of intention. You may sense the intent of your physical body, your emotional body, or even the intentions of specific organs within your body. You may even sense the embodied intentions of your community or your culture. Some intentions may only be sensed as a whisper at the edge of your awareness, such as the mineral desires of the individual molecules in the cells of your body. No matter which intentions manifest, you can respond congruently and consciously one moment at a time.

As I continue to open to intuition, I become more aware how everything I experience is in some way related to my intent. I sense and respond to something that is happening before I rationally know it.

In my hypnosis practice, I see this change happening. Sometimes I will feel a physical or emotional shift while I'm waiting for a client. I may feel tired, excited or even physically uncomfortable. If I allow myself to be present with these feelings, they move through me. Sometimes more information comes and I gain insight about the feeling. Then when my client comes and begins to share his energy with me, I see a connection to what I'm already feeling and more resources become available for our session.

When you notice a change manifesting in your awareness, ask yourself, "What does this change mean?" Then let go and expect an answer. Pay attention to your inner experience. If the change you noticed initially carries more information, it will come. If there is something else you want to know, ask yourself that question, let go, and wait to see what manifests. You can ask, "Is this important? Is this me or someone else?"

Even if what you are experiencing is entirely about you, it may also relate to something larger than you. Both can be true at the same time.

You can invite a synchronous connection with the universe.

As in hypnagogic experiences, the imagery or symbols that spontaneously arrive in our consciousness may have many levels of meaning. They may be multidimensional. The full interpretation of your experience may involve a loosening of ego and inviting unconscious or even superconscious capacities to become present.

Imagine how your life could be moving, evolving, even dancing simultaneously on many levels.
Imagine all the interconnections you are immersed within.

How do you sense those connections?

Become aware of the events in your life that lead to this moment.
Is it possible there are other, subtler intentions related to what you're experiencing now?

Chapter 19

Body Focus as Exploration

Each time you go through the body focus you build on your self awareness. This practice is a meditative pathway into present moment awareness. Each time you go into the body focus you are creating flexibility, shifting from mental doing into receptive, sensory awareness.

> *Take a moment and review what you wrote for several of your body focuses.*
> *Be aware as you're reading them, how they make you feel.*
> *There may be more information contained in what you've written.*
> *Be open for that.*
> *Do it now.*

Reviewing your writing allows your conscious mind to build a framework around what you've been experiencing. Every day or so, go back and look at what you wrote a few days before. You may see deeper insights or symbolic meanings in what you've written. You may also see correlations to things that happened to you later. Your body focus can be precognitive or carry deeper levels of meaning.

Reviewing what you've written can give you a clearer perspective of the process of your awareness.

Do you notice in your previous body focus sessions that there's one sense that comes easier for you?
Is there one that is more difficult?

Do you start with one sense when you are calm, and another when you are agitated?
Do you notice any progressive changes occurring as you do each one?

When you reread your material, you can ask yourself similar questions. Everything you've written can take on new meaning as you ask questions and respond again. You may experience an intuitive sense of your own self in process.

If you haven't done it yet, revisit what you've written.
See where it takes you.

Even if you find your body focus an easy process, take some extra time to sense your shift to deeper receptivity. The more you map the qualities of your shift, the easier and more spontaneous it will become. You will be more able to enter into an intuitive space at will.

When you sense a subtle shift pulling you away from reading, you can soften your mind and body, and see where it leads.

As your body focus gets easier, you can go deeper into one sensation than you normally would. One sensation may even open spontaneously, as a response to some other intent you have. As you open into a color, a shape or a sound, your awareness may shift suddenly into a feeling that has a deeper emotional meaning. The sensations you experience may behave like dreaming imagery; they may be the stirring solicitations of your larger self bringing you more meaning.

So when these unconscious solicitations arise, you can ask yourself what are its intentions? How is my psyche trying to move or shift through this experience? Rather than viewing these expressions as just psychological phenomena, we can ask what the goal is, as if there are deeper intentions within us. You can ask yourself, what is this movement of my being demanding of me? There are many times when you must act on your intuitions, insights and knowings in order to stay congruent with yourself.

As you attend to the intentions of your larger self, you may find that distractions, discomforts and other energies contain information. They may disturb your conscious direction and focus, but they lead to something larger. Any change that "just arrives" in your consciousness may be such an opening.

Is one of your senses speaking to you now?
If so, then take a minute and let that unknown into your awareness.
See where it leads.
Invite that different intelligence to enter your conscious experience.

Pleasure is also unconscious guidance. If there's nothing you're sensing now that you enjoy, then do something to give yourself pleasure.

Start something you enjoy.
Light a scented candle, change the view, put on a sweater...

Your body and mind are intimately connected. If you're struggling against something in your body, what do you suppose is happening to your mind? Be proactive. Move towards what you want. Let pleasure be your ally.

So now go back to whatever it is that you enjoy.
Take a moment now and enjoy it again.

If you're eating something or listening to music while you're reading, then slow down and enjoy it. Give that experience more of your attention. Let the non-rational part of your being lead you for a few moments. Giving attention to your senses will balance you. When you come back to the written word, you will have more internal connection.

Enjoying the Present Moment

Stopping to enjoy something is a natural way to shift from doing to being. Enjoying the pleasure of what is happening takes us out of our minds and validates another level of awareness in us that says, "Be present, and, from this present moment, respond." Enjoyment is an ideomotor doorway to deeper connection with yourself.

> *Again, stop and attend to what is in you.*
> *Allow your inside to guide you.*
> *Be aware of your inner self as it manifests in you.*

Your right response in this moment may be doing nothing. As you rest in the present, it may take time for your body/mind to become more quiet. When you move into stillness, subtler messages arise into consciousness. Each moment of attention directed inwards moves you towards greater connection with your unconscious parts. If in some way you become uncomfortable, you can take care of yourself.

> *So as you sink into a sensation, you can allow it to guide you.*
> *Take your time.*
> *Enjoy.*

> *You can close your eyes if you like.*
> *If emotions come, that's OK too.*
> *You can let go and become more connected with yourself.*

> *Pay attention. Then describe.*
> *Do it again.*

As I write now, I become aware of a pleasant heaviness in my body. As soon as I notice it, I allow my shoulders to relax. Then my breathing deepens a little and I become aware of my lunch sitting heavy in my stomach. As soon as I recognize that heaviness, I realize this feeling has been with me for some time, but I hadn't really noticed it.

Now I want to keep some awareness in my stomach area even as I continue writing. That awareness grounds me. It makes my thinking more digestive, moving without words. I allow some of my awareness to stay with that feeling down in my stomach. It takes me in so easily I feel I would like more time without thoughts, without mental processing. So I'll close my eyes for a time and rest in my body awareness...

Where does your body take you?
As you pay attention to your own sensations you can respond.
You may even pause in between this sentence and the next...

.... and go deeper.

As you stay with what is flowing through you, your awareness will change. You will change. You are a process of change. With practice, you can even allow the temporary discomfort that comes with not knowing, which will bring you new insight and experience. Becoming aware of my stomach was uncomfortable. At first it felt like indigestion. My first response was, "Why would I want to feel that?" As I stayed with it and allowed it, my discomfort released. As I allowed my body to lead me and my mind/body connection become more fluid. When I let go of what I believe I'm supposed to be doing, I move into clear intention.

The movements I experienced are an intuitive response to my digestive sense. There may even be more meaning if I stay with my digestive sensations longer. Any perception, whether it arises from known or unknown causes can be allowed to flow into awareness.

So again, as you are reading, you have choices:

You can attend to your present experience.
You can let it guide you.

You may even allow awkwardness.

This moment might take you away from this book.
You can always come back to these words when your inner flow leads you back to the page.

Wherever you are drawn now, enjoy yourself.
When you're done, describe your experience.

Sound Perception

Focus now on your sense of sound. Read through this exercise first. Then experience it. You don't have to go anywhere or change anything. In fact doing it spontaneously wherever you are can expand your awareness of sound even more.

Right now, as you are reading, there are sounds in the background. Even if you are in an absolutely "quiet" room, there is still some sound, even if it's only sound inside your ears. What you hear now will be your entry point into another kind of awareness.

First, return to your breath.
Enjoy the feeling of your breath flowing in and out.

As you continue breathing, allow your awareness to focus on the sounds you hear.
Any thoughts that flow through your mind are fine.
They can pass right through.
Your focus can stay with the sound your are sensing.
Allow your sense of sound to fill your awareness.

As you keep your focus there, invite any alterations that start to occur in your awareness.
Initially you may become aware of different qualities of sound, more detail, or perhaps more depth.
Other sounds may become conscious.
There may also be changes in other senses or in your body.
While focusing on sound, your inner attention will begin to shift in some way.

This sense is a doorway to your unconscious.

At some point, when you begin to notice a shift in your awareness, imagine that your entire sense of sound is becoming a portal.
Open that doorway and pass through into a more direct connection with your unconscious.
Enjoy where that connection takes you.
Take as long as your unconscious needs.
Allow it to lead you with intelligence, gentleness and patience.

When you're ready, you can come back to your normal awareness.
Allow any interesting sensations to remain—long enough to be recognized by your conscious mind.
When you're done, return fully to your normal awareness.

You can remember what you've experienced.
You can describe your experience.

Do it now.

Going into the sound, you may have experienced a change in emotion, thoughts or even body sensations. Since those arrivals weren't intentionally created by your conscious mind, they probably came from your unconscious. With practice, you can allow your awareness to flow wherever it needs to go. What you experience will become meaningful.

Pause...

You can remember and revisit things you enjoy.

Fascination - What fascinates you and captivates your attention is a direct expression of your deepest intentions. Follow those intentions into a deeper discovery of your self.

Drawing textures - Extend your non-linear communication. Draw experiences that are not visual. There are unlimited ways to communicate your experience.

Newspaper - Practice extending your intuition and intention daily. Use the main photo or story each day in the newspaper as a precognitive exercise. Get feedback.

Affirmations - Talk to yourself with words that move you towards your deepest goals. Speak from the feeling of being connected with yourself. You can manifest what you want, using the conscious and unconscious parts of yourself.

Sound Focus - You can use any sense as a doorway into trance. Allow your focus to go as deep as you wish. Trust your own trance-formation.

Chapter 20

State Markers

Your practice of attending to your deeper intentions builds bridges between ways of being and ways of thinking that have been shut off from your normal consciousness. Inviting unexpected solicitations allows your subtle inner messenger to speak. That messenger is the unconscious, or through the unconscious, higher consciousness, spirit, or spirit guides. When I open up to this other intelligence it sometimes feels like a separate presence. Other times it's more internally connected and feels like a familiar part of me. When I sense I'm in a meaningful connection with myself or something larger that myself, I try to be conscious of the felt sense of where I am. This "state" awareness helps me build conscious awareness. I know when I'm shifting and where I am at any given moment.

This afternoon, I took some time to do an intentional intuitive practice. I did the body focus, then some sensory imagining as I focused on my breath. These practices relaxed my mind and body. At this point I had a sense of myself in the midst of a space which extended outwards from me in all directions. I know this space I sense is more than a physical space when I'm experiencing it. It's a meaningful, altered state of mind. I now recognize this state of awareness as similar to the hypnagogic state, that threshold place between waking and sleep. When I am there my intention is not to go to sleep, and I don't become sleepy. I value the experience of this flow state and the deeper connection I feel with myself. When I start to perceive that sense of space I experience a connection to what I perceive as larger parts of my self, expansive non-ego parts.

By attending to yourself, you can learn to recognize your own markers or access points into these other ways of being and knowing. With each body focus you do, the markers of your own conscious shifting will become more conscious. You may notice how a particular body part relaxes. Perhaps you feel a shift where you normally hold tension. You may notice how your mood shifts subtly. You might experience a change in the sensitivity of one or all of your senses. As you start to identify these markers, you will also recognize how often you are spontaneously going in and out of light trance states throughout your day.

Remembering one of these markers then becomes a way to consciously shift your awareness. In hypnosis, anchoring is a way to use the markers consciously. When you put your body into a particular position you will reconnect to the feelings and the awareness you had the last time you were in the same position. This remembering is similar to what happens when you hear the name of a good friend. The body memories associated with the name become instantly available to you again. If you spontaneously touch your heart with your hand when you remember that person, that touch becomes an anchor.

> **If you spontaneously touch your heart with your hand when you remember that person, that touch becomes an anchor.**

This spontaneous movement is often done unconsciously, but you can use it to reactivate the feelings and memories associated with that person. Another common way you might experience a state marker is connected to your sleep pattern. If you lie down at the end of your day, you may remember a feeling or a dream image from the morning. When you recline, you reconnect with recent or meaningful sensations you had in the same position. Similarly, you may remember a dream in the morning, if you roll back into the position you were in when you were sleeping.

In some of my deeper explorations of consciousness, the stillness of my body becomes my anchor. The calmness that surrounds me as I drift into the hypnagogic state becomes the entry point for my awareness. My conscious awareness goes other places, but my body's quietness and stability becomes the ground connection for a deep flow of consciousness. On the flip side, my body also directs the flow of my awareness towards integration, literally pulling my consciousness back into my body with a twitch or an itch.

Can you remember the felt sense of your own inner shift?
What happens if you allow your body to go with that shift?
What position does your body want to flow into?

Are there other body positions that are related to other states of mind?

Take notes.
While you write and remember, notice the connection between your body and what flows into your awareness.

Psychometry

Similarly, a physical contact through one of the senses can open the door to a flow of information from the unconscious or the higher consciousness. You can touch an object, an artifact or any physical object and have access to energy or information connected to it. This skill, called psychometry, is one of the oldest and most direct ways of accessing intuition.

Psychometry may be a form of homeopathic sensitivity, an ability to pick up traces left within an object, traces that are so negligible as to be unmeasurable. I suspect though that there may be no physical explanation for it. It may be just that we inhabit experiencing bodies and we respond well to touch. When we extend our hand to touch something, we become receptive. That may be the key.

The late intuitive archaeologist George McMullen had a talent for psychometrizing artifacts. When McMullen first met the Canadian archaeologist, Norman Emerson, he psychometrized some artifacts while sitting at Emerson's kitchen table. Emerson described this:

> *I presented George with a fragment of an artifact from the Black Creek site located in metropolitan Toronto. He held the fragment in his hand, contemplated it, fondled it, and meditated on it at length. He then correctly told me it was a pipe stem, told me the age of the site it came from, and told me the location of the site. He described how the pipe was manufactured, described the maker, and provided details about the community and living conditions. He then took pencil and paper in hand and drew a picture of the pipe bowl, which he stated belonged to the broken pipe stem.*
> *"I was fascinated and impressed because I immediately recognized that he had clearly drawn a picture of a typical Iroquois conical ring bowl pipe. This type of pipe was one of the popular types recovered from the Black Creek Site...* [23]

McMullen went on to accurately psychometrize several other of Emerson's artifacts. McMullen's success so impressed Emerson that he dedicated a large portion of the rest of his life to working with McMullen and promoting intuitive archaeology.

McMullen said he was able to connected with the energy that was left in the object by whomever used it or created it. He had learned his own internal process of being receptive to that information. He had a remarkable ability to read almost any kind of energetic event from the history of an object. His work is well documented in his book, <u>One White Crow</u> [23] and in Stephen Schwartz' book, <u>The Alexandria Project</u>. [28]

Beverly Jaegers was the director of a volunteer intuitive group called the "Psi Squad" who worked on criminal investigations. The Psi Squad used psychometry as a valuable component of their intuitive explorations. One object she used to train her team was a piece of stone from a massive landslide caused by an earthquake in

Montana. She felt it was one of her best targets because of the raw energy it contained. I appreciate this example because it illustrates how just about any kind of energetic event can be perceived, not just an event containing human activity.

The information that is "read" in psychometry may be determined by the intensity of the events associated with it as well as the sensitivity or inclinations of the intuitive. Jaegers stated how objects fresh from a crime scene were often the most effective for producing psychic information about the crime. These impressions are accessible to any person open to perceiving other levels of information. Jaegers said:

> *In testing people I have not found any (students) who could not learn to extend the sense of touch to do psychic touch or psychometry. I have also trained people who felt that they could "hear" or it seemed they could. However, it did not change the fact that they did this hearing by first touching the item in one way or another, with the hand for the most part, and in some cases, just touching it with the mind.* [20]

This last statement seems to hint that if it is an energy that makes psychometry possible, it may be transferred more like a thought than a physical energy. All that is necessary is to have a pointer to what you are targeting. Even a photocopy of a photograph when touched can release information.

Psychometry may be more effective for people who are kinesthetically inclined. Again, Jaegers felt that psychometry,

> *...does indeed deal with some anomalous energy that seems to be somehow absorbed by and integrated into, an object... How you perceive that information is where we dip into the other field. We can use an object as a hard-target. The target itself is the launch-pad for the remote viewing. You know nothing about the object. Using the mere "touch" of the object as a place to begin a remote viewing is a huge push of the envelope.* [20]

With a physical object, there's no doubt where we are starting.

However, you are going beyond the physical with your intent. You resonate in a non-conscious way to a larger "field" of information that goes way beyond the physical.

Playing with Objects

Once you've initiated your practice of intuition through sensory awareness, it's an easy step to begin exploring objects with your intuitive senses. You can begin with things around your work or at home. The important thing is to work with objects where you can get feedback. Lyall Watson offers a simple exercise you can use to practice with family or friends:

> *Get them to go out and select a local stone, small enough to carry and appealing enough to make them want to handle it often. Then, at the end of the week, have each of the objects placed into an identical sealed envelope and brought to you. See if you can tell which belongs to each of the individuals involved. Open the envelope and handle the objects if you must, but by the third or fourth trial you will find that you do not need to do that to get most of the answers right.* [33]

Again if you play with these intuitive games, take time to get good feedback. Connect with the person involved with his object. As you connect, you will start to recognize an energy or a quality that is different with each person. You can sense this energy just by handling the person's object.

Obviously, any objects can be chosen. With stones you may be able to deduct who would choose each one. Stones on the other hand, do give you more personal interest. The person carrying it might enjoy the feeling of a stone more than a domino. So why not make it fun for them too?

This exercise is a really good one for contrasts. You may get perceptions from one object, that taken alone you might not recognize. When you move to the second object, then you can perceive a difference. Often you may not have even recognized what you were sensing with the first object until you start in on the second. Then you will realize, "Oh, this one is different..." and you'll be aware what you were sensing from the first. If this is the case, certainly go back and add your first perceptions to the first object. Also, as you see these contrasts, you may then see how your perceptions relate to differences you've recognized between people.

When you do psychometry, you may have intuitive perceptions through any of your senses and through thoughts or feelings. Touch only serves as the starting point. Any change you experience anywhere in your being may be an intuitive response. One of the challenges with using an object is that we may get caught or fixated on the physical, because our minds want something tangible to focus on when we're seeking information. Yet, if we stay with the physical, we will only perceive what our physical senses give us. So here, your experience with sensing, using the mandala, or even working with sounds will be helpful. You can let your awareness shift into inner sensing after your initial contact with the physical object. Using uniform objects like dominoes makes this easier, as this gives you less to latch on to with your conscious mind.

> **When you do psychometry, you may have intuitive perceptions through any of your senses, thoughts or feelings. Touch only serves as the starting point.**

Here's another fun variation so you can work with a neutral object. For this exercise you need a friend.

> *Arrange a meeting time with a friend.*
> *Then each of you independently find a flower. If you can, choose a flower that hasn't even been picked yet, say one in your garden or one growing wild in nature. If you can't find a live one, you can use a flower from a bouquet.*
> *Each of you carries the flower with you as you hold in your mind a question you would like answered or an experience about which you would like more information. This will "imprint" the flower with your energy and the particular focus of your intention.*

When you meet, you can set your flowers on a table in front of or in between each other. Individually calm your minds and center your awareness in the present, recognizing and releasing any energies, emotions, or thoughts you're carrying with you.

Then when you're ready, pick up the other person's flower. Let yourself attune to the energies of the flower and allow yourself to describe any and all experiences you have. Each of you use paper sketching images and describing experiences and perceptions.

Alternately, you could each take turns and describe your perceptions and experiences to the other person. Make sure the person listening takes notes of what is described.

After each person is finished perceiving the flower, then you can share your results with each other. Once again, as your receive the other person's "reading" of your flower, be sure to be open, watching for your own intuitive responses.

Be sure to debrief each other about your intentions and experiences you noticed during the time you were each holding your flower. If you had other emotional or highly energetic events happening to you during the day, your friend might have also picked up on those events!

You can also thank your flowers at the end of your experiment.

Do it now...
Do you have a question on your mind? Or an event you would like another perspective on?
Then ask a friend to play with you!

Here again, the flower opens the door to the other information associated with it. I like this approach because the person perceiving understands that the flower is just the doorway to the information. Thus it's easier for each participant to tune out other information once an energetic connection has been made. Be sure when you get feedback from your friend about his intentions, that you note your own intuitive connections. You can keep learning from your feedback.

There is also interesting research that seems to confirm it's our lived experience with objects that gives them meaning. Objects that haven't been handled or have very little energy invested in them may be harder to perceive with intuition. Watson did an experiment seeing if intuitives could perceive which envelopes contained money and which contained blank slips of paper. They failed miserably differentiating the newly printed money from plain paper, but had no trouble identifying the used money. He also found they were able to sort the identically sized paper money of the United States astonishingly well into piles according to value.

These experiments clearly show how our attitude towards objects in our lives gives them value and meaningfulness. Watson points out in the above experiment that even a forged bill would end up feeling the same way as a bill of equal value once it was treated as a real bill. Money may be particularly useful to practice with because of the high emotional value we give it.

Money Energy

You can set up a simple exercise for yourself. Get a one dollar, a twenty and a hundred dollar bill. Fold each bill into a tri-folded piece of blank paper. Then put each bill into an identical blank security envelope. Shuffle the envelopes. Then have someone else shuffle them. Then when you're ready, lay the three envelopes out on a table in front of you and label them A, B, and C. Soften your mind and your body and move into a receptive state of mind. See if you can sense differences between them.

Are there contrasts between them in texture, temperature, energy or color?

Hold each one individually. Do you feel any different energy in your body with each one? Switch between them and see what differences you sense.

Do any seem more or less interesting to you?

Hold each envelope, one at a time, and ask yourself, "Where

> would this one take me?" or "What would this bring to me?" Then see what comes to mind.
>
> Imagine giving each envelope in turn to a friend, a child, or a stranger. How does each option feel?
>
> Describe all the differences you perceive.
>
> Based on what you've sensed, which one do you feel is the $100, which one the $20, and which one the $1.
>
> When you're done, open the envelopes and enjoy the results.
> Be sure to revisit your perceptions for each envelope now that you know which is which.
> Repeat it as often as you like.

Once you open your awareness to the energies of objects, you can creatively find many different places to practice your sensing abilities. Antique stores are loaded with energized objects. Finding two antiques that are similar can often give you amazing contrasts in energy. Here you probably won't get clear feedback about what caused the differences, but you can sense them just the same. If you actually wanted to purchase an antique, you could then choose one that felt good to you. You can choose the kind of energy you want to take home with you.

The same process comes into play when we handle a sacred object or a family heirloom. We perceive the collective intentions and energies of everyone else who interacted with the object. The sense of awe and a sense of the sacred that comes when we walk into a church is the same psychometric process on a larger scale. The entire building becomes charged with the collective history of the energetic events that have occurred there.

We also have the ability to attune to specific energies depending on our personal interests. The bank teller, a blind person or perhaps a drug dealer may be better than the average person at telling the denominations of bills by touch. In the same way, a religious historian would be attuned to the energies around sacred artifacts.

A Native American elder may be better able to sense which objects are authentic Native American artifacts. Any person has increased sensitivity in the realm where they have personal experience. The auto mechanic will be more likely to know the faulty part from the correct one just by holding it. The woman who knitted her whole life and goes blind can still pick out the matching colors using her sense of touch.

McMullen had an affinity to Native American sites and their energies were easily accessible to him. Curiously, his affinity didn't come through research. He had a strong interest since he was a young boy. Sometimes we're born with sensitivities, and with luck, we are allowed to explore them. So with every exercise you do, pay attention to your affinities. Enjoy them. Explore them.

As with other intuitive exercises, psychometry seems to work best when the conscious mind is relaxed, allowing the unconscious to flow in other directions. When you work in your field of expertise, you already know what you need to do and you relax into it. In fact you may not even realize how you are doing it. If you have a special talent, you are probably already using intuition in various ways.

With psychometry, actually having an object can be captivating. It's easy for the conscious mind to become engaged with the physical qualities of the object. If this happens, let it happen, notice the fascination and interest. Keep in mind your intentions to let other kinds of information come into your awareness. You can let go of the tangible aspects of the object and open the door to other information. Perception begins with your felt shift inwards toward the more subtle, inner senses.

Each body focus serves to cultivate your awareness and sensitivity. With practice, you can be open to your subtle, inner responses to an object, a hand-shake or even a space you walk into. You can perceive what is meaningful to you.

Do a psychometry experiment.
Set up one of the exercises on the previous pages for yourself.
Have fun.

Asking Questions

With psychometry, as with all intuitive exploration, you can ask questions. Who owned this object? Were they male or female, young or old? The receptivity of intuition blends with the curiosity and direction of your normal conscious thinking. With practice, you can encourage a flow between your conscious and unconscious processes. When you want to perceive something, you can express your intent, then relax, and let go. Shift your state of mind and be receptive. You will get a response from your unconscious. You will learn to trust it.

For instance, if you walk into a room and suddenly feel a discomfort in your stomach, you begin your process by recognizing your discomfort. You shift out of what you were "doing" and become more present. Then you wait for some meaning to come. You could check in and see if there are sensations or changes occurring in other channels of perception. You may in that moment enter into a natural flow of information from your unconscious that becomes more meaningful as it evolves.

But what if you become receptive and nothing changes? You can check in with what you need and ask yourself questions.

> *Is this feeling important to me?*
> *Is this feeling from me or is it related to someone in this room?*
> *Is there anything I need to do?*

If there's no response or change to the last question, then let it go. You may be experiencing indigestion and that's all it is. If there is something you need to know, the information will come. The more you trust yourself, the more trustworthy your intuition becomes. With any question you ask, you can slip back into receiving and see what happens.

> *Your unconscious will respond to your intent and your focus and provide you with an answer.*
> *With any information you perceive, you can respond with full conscious awareness in a way that is congruent with all of your being, including your mind, body, heart and spirit.*

Chapter 21

Expanding Visualization

The following visualization exercise can be read by another person for a deeper effect or you can read it to yourself onto a tape. If you read it to yourself in real time, you can shift into a softer, passive focus as you read. Allow your voice to relax. Develop a smooth, relaxed rhythm. Be sure to allow lots of time to experience the words and images. Let the meaning and movement of each phrase move through you before you continue with the next. Your inner sensing will unfold at a slower body-centered pace. Give yourself extra time to experience after any phrase that resonates. You can go into each sensation as deeply as you like. You can even drift away from the words into your own flow.

> *So once again, attend to what you are sensing now.*
> *Become aware of what you see in the space around you.*
>
> *Can you perceive the colors, shapes, textures and qualities of light without labeling?*
>
> *Become aware of other sensations.*
> *What are you smelling, tasting, hearing and feeling with your body?*

Take some time and pay attention to each sense in the same receptive manner.

As you attend to each sensation, you become more present.
Quieter perceptions will come into your awareness as you become more quiet and more receptive.
Allow for that subtlety as you settle deeper into your experience.

Become aware of the air that is all around you.
Enjoy that surrounding presence.

Your gaze can soften.
Your hearing and your feelings can soften as well—all the senses softening and blending.
You can allow all your senses to equalize and become balanced.
Imagine them all blending and entwining.
Allow all your senses to settle into a shared presence.

As this happens, become aware of your breathing.
Let your breath flow in and out as it is.
There is no need to alter it, or resist it.
Your breath can flow in and out at whatever speed or depth feels right to your body.
You can observe and allow.

Then from within the flow of your experience, you can expand your senses.
Imagine, with your eyes open, that you can extend your awareness out further.
You can sense through and beyond the walls of the room you are in.
You can do this in whatever way feels comfortable to you.
You may feel, see or hear with an expanded sense outward around you.
Allow yourself to imagine that awareness.

Enjoy it.
You may begin with what you know is out beyond those walls, bringing those perceptions into you.

Take your time.
Enjoy your inner senses expanding.

You can extend your awareness creatively.
You can allow your sensations to become clearer.
You can flow with each sensation you experience.
Your body may move; your breathing may change.
Your eyes can be open or closed.
It can all happen in this flow of allowing and unfolding.

When you feel comfortable, you can slowly extend your imagining outwards, even further away... into the distance.
Expand your field of experience.
Allow yourself to sense this expansion.
Any sounds?
Other sensations?
Where does this flow take you?

Then, as your awareness continues to expand, begin to sense the topography that surrounds you.
You can sense the shape of the land that supports all the human activities around you.
Is there a valley that your awareness sweeps out into?
An open plain? A river? A mountain?
How do you perceive these larger forms?

Do you notice feelings, images, sounds, or a combination of senses?
What does the air outside feel like?
Does it change in temperature as you expand?
Does the light become brighter or darker?
Are there energetic differences?

*Imagine that a physical part of you is extending out into all of
   this space.*
*Part of you is extending with your senses and your
   imagination and touches everything you perceive and
   imagine.*
Enjoy that connection.

The larger part of you becomes more real as you enjoy it.
*Along with this expanded awareness, you can also be aware of
   your physical body.*
Both aspects can be shared equally in your awareness.

How do you sense that larger part of you?
Is it familiar?
*These larger sensations become an opening for a larger way
   of being.*

*Staying in your flow, you can allow yourself to extend
   all the way out to the farthest horizon, expanding and
   encompassing everything you pass.*
As far as you go, a sense of you always remains in the center.
*The physical horizon all around you now forms the outer edge
   of your being.*
Enjoy all the expansiveness of yourself.

Breathe into that expansiveness.

Take your time.

Enjoy the sensations as long as you wish.
*The felt sense you have now connects you with a larger part of
   yourself.*

You can explore this awareness in a playful way.
Do you have a desire to move?
Allow that.
How about altering this larger body in some way?

How about changing your perspective?
Follow your creativity.
You can shift to the center again while the rest of you remains expanded.
Describe your experiences to yourself. Write down your experiences and perceptions.
Describe them in detail.
Sketch images or feelings you perceived.
Allow your awareness to flow into the describing of everything you recall.
Take your time.

You can stay in the flow of your experience as you describe.

As you come back into your body, it may need to move.
Allow that.
You can continue reading this text when you are moved to do so.

You don't need an actual perception of space to make your imagining work. If you imagine space, you experience the same results. That was the reason I asked you to imagine yourself extending out beyond your walls.

Personally, when I imagine space, I perceive it as a felt sense at the edge of my skin. That tactile sense is a contact point for me. That point can be focused, objectified and tangible. From there, if allowed, it will unfold into a more diffuse opening up. I have to shift how I am attending to experience the shift in my awareness.

When we imagine space, we make an effort to imagine the unimaginable, to perceive what is not known. You can step off the cliff and learn to love that moment of absolutely not knowing. When you allow yourself to let go into the stepping, you create something to step onto. It is an edge to the conscious mind, an edge to what we know, and it can be scary until we shift our perspective.

Extending outwards we touch the edge of ego and conscious identity. We reach that edge any time we extend towards creativity, intuition or inspiration. Learning to live with intuitive awareness is about learning to live life at that edge of conscious control. However we experience these edges, we can respect and validate them as openings, doorways, potentials for new experiences.

Then we need to return to the center and to what is known. We allow ourselves to come together and integrate. The tangible and physical provide a framework for the rest of our experience. The edges make our framework larger.

Immersed Experience and Flow

When we take the time to sense something as simple as the table top, we begin to experience reciprocity between ourselves and the rest of the sensuous world. It is an intimate connection. More importantly, we sense everything within us, within our sense of self and within the realm of our experience. When we really taste an apple, we are filled with it. To the degree that we open ourselves to it, we can merge with appleness—the richness of taste, texture, smell and sound. That's when intuitions enter. We apprehend more than is knowable through a detached mind.

When our attention is narrow focused, it is only the "I am" part or the ego that is in consciousness. (See figure 6 on page 82.) Here the realm of conscious material is dominant. This is the Beta brain wave state where willing and striving are dominant. The Beta frequencies behave like a closed loop, and the threshold between conscious and unconscious processes is not permeable.

When our awareness becomes more immersed and diffuse, unconscious information including creativity, intuition and higher consciousness becomes accessible. Other brain wave frequencies like Alpha and Theta manifest. The threshold between the conscious and unconscious is more permeable.

All the exercises in this book are intended to help you loosen those boundaries and build pathways between the different parts of yourself. When our intellects are balanced with the experiencing body, then the full depth of our potential becomes more readily available. We can perceive directly, act on it consciously, and even engage analytically with it. All this happens in a state of flow.

That flow state is what I call clear intent. When all of our intentions and all of the parts of ourselves are working together, we experience the unimpeded flow of consciousness. It is also a trance, at least until it becomes a more accepted part of our conscious being. The state of flow can be truly powerful and transformative. Do you want to limit your experience to what is known, or do you want to open up to an intelligence and experience that is much larger than your conscious mind? As James Carse said in his beautiful book, Finite and Infinite Games:

> *To be prepared against surprise is to be trained. To be prepared for surprise is to be educated.* [10]

I believe if you educate yourself about your own altered states, you can utilize this ability to merge with experience. Altered states hold a key to truly experiencing and knowing the expanded world. Every time you allow yourself to "go into" a sensation with awareness, you are learning how to cultivate your own flow state in a healthy, dynamic way.

Chapter 22

Intention and Body

Each time you enjoy the richness of now, each time you explore your own depth with a meditation, a sensory awareness practice, or an intuitive exercise, you become more able to shift from knowing to being and perceiving. Staying present becomes more challenging when the feelings or sensations are stronger, more charged with emotion. These challenging moments lead to profound transformation as you stay present with yourself.

Here's an exercise to build awareness of the balance point between intention and expectation. Read this exercise through first:

> *Hold an arm out in front of you, palm up.*
> *Close your eyes.*
> *Become aware of the tip of your middle finger.*
> *Become aware what your are sensing in your finger.*
> *In the same way become aware of the skin on the tip of your nose. Then think about touching the tip of your nose with your middle finger.*
>
> *Then SLOWLY, start moving your hand toward your face, bending at the elbow.*
> *Do this very slowly.*

Can you be continuously aware of the relationship between your nose and your finger?

Pause your hand movement for a moment as it is moving closer and slowly move your head from side to side.
Attune yourself to the relationship between your finger and nose as you move your head.
Does this movement change your sense of your finger, nose, or the relationship between them?

Slowly continue moving your hand and arm again.
Sense the relationship, as these two parts of your body become closer.
Stop again when you suspect your hand is quite close.
Does your awareness change if you move your head around again?
What do you sense?
Follow your awareness with sensitivity and attention until you experience a direct sense of touch somewhere between your face and your hand.

Be aware of your feelings, thoughts and energies throughout.

Then describe your experience.

Do it now.

Afterwards notice your reactions. Did your hand touch your face where you thought it would? How did what you thought was happening relate to what you were feeling? The differences between what you thought was happening and what was happening can be very informative. Was there a difference? Were you able to sense anything in your face or your hand before they physically touched?

You can do this exercise again or several times. Do it to heighten your sensitivity and to increase your mind/body coordination. You can switch hands and notice the difference. When you feel your hand and face are almost touching, then pause and slowly move your head around. With practice, you will begin to sense where your hand is, which will be different than where you think it is. You can allow that sensitivity to guide you. Hold your awareness on what you sense rather than what you think and allow the hand to move closer and touch. It takes effort to focus and to be in your body so intentionally. You will sharpen your intention and your ability to stay in the present.

> *Do this exercise again now, perhaps using your other hand. Afterwards, describe your perceptions and experiences.*
> *Did you experience any interesting sensations?*
> *Describe the connection between your mind and your body during that exercise.*
> *Does this exercise put you into a different kind of trance? If so, how do you sense it?*

You can extend your awareness similarly into other parts of your body. Some areas will be much more connected to conscious intention than others. Awareness will come easier in those areas, but you may also have a harder time truly being present there. If you are familiar expressing intention with a part of your body, it can be more challenging to receive with that part.

Discovering Unconscious Intentions

As soon as we start to pay attention to our bodies, we very often come up against unexpected sensations, discomforts or messages. These manifestations may be unconscious messages that haven't yet been recognized consciously. In a sense, they're backed up, waiting for recognition. This backup may be perceived in many ways. You may feel tired, tense or in pain. You may also experience excessive energy or even a lack of sensation in some part of your body.

> *Stress in the body is the physical manifestation of a blocked unconscious intention.*

Unconscious messages become stronger and stronger until they are recognized and acted upon. When you begin an intuitive process, you will first have to recognize and release these subtle messages in your body/mind. Any stress held in the body will have a tendency to override other, more subtle information arising from the unconscious.

For instance, the first response some of my clients have during a hypnotherapy session is to fall asleep. Their unconscious expressed rest as a primary need. Consciously they may have something else in mind, but their body and unconscious override their intentions. If they are under a lot of stress, it may take some time before we can get to the conscious issue they intend to explore. That being said, underlying stress may also relate to their presenting issue. Many people have no idea what the wholeness of their body/mind needs. For example a person may be sleep deprived but honestly think they are perfectly rested.

When you develop sensory awareness and presence you relive your stress. As you practice, your unconscious stresses become more easily conscious. The intentions behind them come to the surface and release. More often relieving stress isn't about doing something, but about not doing and allowing the unconscious to lead. Shifting to "not doing" may lead to sleep, to daydreaming, and even to an emotional release. As you become more aware of your entire being, you will sense the signals of stress in your body sooner. You can be present with these signals and respond in a loving way.

> More often relieving stress isn't about doing something, but about not doing and allowing the unconscious to lead.

For me, stress often shows up in my lower back. When I'm overly focused on my writing or some other cognitive task, the sensations in my back progressively get stronger and stronger. When I'm focused solely on my work, I sense a vague discomfort and may shift my physical position without really paying attention. The feeling may subside for a few moments, but doesn't go away. It will return a little stronger a short time later. The longer I ignore this message, the more "painful" it becomes. I will actually throw my back out if I ignore the signals for days on end. Then I'm forced to stop everything else and deal with my body, as if it's a rebellious child.

When I stop and attend consciously to what is happening in my body, things immediately begin to shift. I become aware I am feeling sensations. I go into them and allow them. I may even have a short, releasing emotional response. As this happens, I'll have an impulse to sit up straighter and breathe deeper into my chest and abdomen. Suddenly I feel my toes again, and more energy returns to my body. In this allowing flow, I might sense a need for a longer break, perhaps a walk and more deep breathing.

The solution or message of a stressful symptom is in the symptom. The challenge is to let go of whatever you thought was important and attend to the messages already in your body. With intuitive practice, you learn to value this other way of knowing and being. As you develop your sensitivity and your openness, you can follow any sensation to its source by allowing your unconscious to lead.

Chapter 23

Breathing into the Body

Bring your awareness into your body now as you read this text.
Soften your eyes.
Sit up straight so you can breathe easily.
Take in a nice deep breath; then purse your lips like you're blowing through a straw.
Exhale all the air out slowly through your lips.
Do this several times.
There's no need to retain the air. You can allow it to cycle all the way in or out.

Pay attention to the sensation of the air passing through your lips. You'll notice as you attend to the breath, that its rhythm changes.
Your awareness changes with it.
You can enjoy the feeling of your changing breath.
It will guide you.
With each breath you allow with full awareness you are learning a tangible way to release tension and stress.
As you breathe, you can allow your awareness to move around inside your body.

*Notice what sensations and feelings you encounter in your
    body.
When you become aware of a particular spot, perhaps
    one that's uncomfortable, painful or new, imagine each
    incoming breath going into that spot and filling it up.*

*Then with each exhale, you can allow the flowing breath to
    relax and release what you're sensing in that spot.
This may amplify a sensation or diminish it.
You can flow with the breath and become present with the
    intentions underneath that sensation.
Let your body respond to your loving attention.
Allow the body to move if it needs to.*

*As you're breathing with the sensations in your body, you
    might have intuitive responses in your other senses.
What does the breath look like as it leaves you?
What colors do your body sensations have?
Do they have sounds?
Textures?
Shapes?
As you allow these other senses to respond, you are accessing
    the information encoded in your body sensations.
This information may or may not make sense to your
    conscious mind.
You can still allow its meaning to inform you.*

*As your breathing releases the stress in your body, it will shift
    your body, your heart, perhaps your whole awareness.
You can do anything you need to do in response to what you're
    feeling.*

*You can be present with yourself as you release stress.
You can be present with yourself as you become a congruent
    flow of conscious and unconscious intentions.
Take some time and breathe now.*

Often when people practice this inner breath releasing, they find that they become more energized and active. Relieving stress may not be a sedating process. I will emphasize the activating part of breath releasing again:

Relieving stress may be an activating experience.

Stress is often thought of as a too-much-going-on phenomena. But it can equally result from not doing something important. When you begin listening to your unconscious intentions, you may feel a need for movement or expression. Stress can also caused by internal pressures you create within yourself. Any time you hold on to something in any way, you create stress.

Make one of your hands into a fist.
Hold it.
Keep the muscles tight.
If you continue holding it, you will feel fatigue.
How long does it take?

Let the hand relax.
Feel how good it feels to let go.

Conversely, you can let your hand lie totally quiet.
Give it time to fall asleep, becoming inert and heavy.

Then, at some point, the expression of that hand's intention
    will suggest movement.
Keeping your hand from moving will build pressure inside you.
When you finally move your hand again, you will have a
    wonderful feeling of letting go.

Any mental or emotional holding will create similar fatigue and stress. Our tendency as a culture is to be in a narrow, objective focus. We're often focused totally on one thing, though we may jump from one to the other if we're multi-tasking. We have a clear sense of the object of our focus being outside of us. Our way of attending to the world allows us to have a high efficiency, task oriented lifestyle. We are very productive. Unfortunately, when we stay in this narrow focus all the time, we create stress. We do not recognize or utilize the dynamic flexibility and strength of the mind/body system that we live in.

> *If you hold your attention focused for too long, you experience stress, regardless of the content of your attention.*

You can even be too fixated on the idea of relaxation and never experience it, until you come into your body and actually feel it. As I mentioned, changing the way you are attending can immediately reduce your stress level. That's what the breathing does. It shifts you from a narrow mental focus, like reading, to an immersed and more diffuse sensation in the body. The degree to which you can immerse yourself in the feeling of relaxing, the greater shift you will experience and the greater the relief and pleasure. Relieving stress is a pleasurable experience because you are coming back into a larger sense of yourself.

Body Touch

Another technique that works well is self-massage. Read through this exercise first.

> *Close your eyes.*
> *Take both hands and gently lay your palms on your face covering your eyes, but not resting on the eyes.*
> *Put the heels of your palms on your cheekbones and your fingers up over your forehead.*
> *Leave your nose uncovered so you can breathe easily.*
> *Feel the contact of your hands on your face.*
> *Enjoy this feeling for a minute or two.*
> *Feel the warmth that builds between your hands and the muscles of your face.*
> *Breath into that comfortable feeling.*
>
> *Notice how you can open and close your eyes and still*

experience relaxation.
If you see any light, adjust your hands to block it out.
Allowing your eyes to be open in blackness and warmth is very relaxing.
You can give your eyes the gift of not needing to see.
They can relax and remember truly letting go.

Then, at some point, let your eyes close again.
Gently start moving your hands and fingers.
Move your hands while focusing on the sensation of the touch, rather than from the idea of touching yourself.
Can you sense what feels good rather than what you think should feel good?
You can increase the pressure in one place or touch more lightly in another.
Move softly and slowly and pay attention to what you feel in your hands and face.
Explore the feeling from within your felt sense of the touch.
You may find your body wants to move to another position as you explore.
Let yourself respond with enjoyment and pleasure.

Let your hands move all over your face, let them roam, perhaps around the sides of your head, even around your neck and shoulders.
Go slowly and gently.
If you find a sensitive or painful spot, go even slower.
Breathe into it.
Press in gently and notice what happens.
Let your hands rest in that spot and notice what happens.

Your presence will transform the sensations in your body.
Continue inhaling and exhaling in a comfortable, present way.
Then when you feel you've gone far enough, open your eyes and take a deep breath. Stretch your arms and shoulders and become aware of the room around you.

Do it now.

Afterwards, take a moment and check-in with yourself.
How do you feel?
Do you perceive any differences in your vision?
How about your other senses?
Do you experience changes in your mind, heart, body or spirit?
Be aware of any other changes you experience, and recognize and validate them.
Describe them to yourself.

Allow that softness in your body as you continue...

Touch takes you out of narrow, objective focus. This shift may be profound if narrow mental focus is your habitual way of being and attending. The five minutes or so it takes to stop and attend to yourself repays you with an increase in energy, heightened creativity and even clearer thinking. When you have shifted into a different state, you can return to the tasks at hand with more energy, presence, and intuitive insight. The self massage activity is part of a routine for improving vision. Teaching your eyes how to relax and shift to soft focus leads to improved vision. Often, after resting the eyes, your vision will be sharper, focusing will be easier and the colors will be brighter. See Aldous Huxley's book, <u>The Art of Seeing</u> [18] for more information on these techniques.

Refining Senses

Now, do a body focus. Become aware of what you are feeling or sensing, inside or out. Check into all your senses, thoughts and feelings.

Allow enough time with each sense to go deeper into your present awareness.

Describe what you experience as accurately as you can.
Be attentive to differences that show up and describe them.
Do it now.

Afterwards, look over what you have written. Is there a predominant sensation? When you do the body focus, you might center your awareness around one sense or a constellation of senses. Each time you do your body focus you are building your understanding of your baseline. From there you can watch the changes that occur spontaneously within you any time during the day.

Take a moment and read through several of your body focuses. Notice which one of your senses gets little attention or ends up last on the list. Which sense has the least number of words associated with it? You may find several senses that get little attention. The following exercise will increase your awareness of these unused senses. Read through this exercise first:

Take a few moments more and attend to one of your lesser used senses.
Notice what, if anything you are already perceiving with that sense.
Give yourself permission to stay with your perception a little longer.
Be patient with yourself.

You may feel uncertainty, awkwardness or even discomfort.
You can be present with those feelings.

Anything you sense will be a doorway into deeper awareness of yourself.
See where your experiencing body is leading you.

Since you don't have a good rapport with this sense, it will be easier to move into the unknown of immediate perception.
The awkwardness or unfamiliarity may be valuable.
With this sense, you have an opportunity to truly experience without your mind's filter.

Now explore your environment using this sense.
For example, if the sense you want to enliven is smell, then

start smelling things. Smell several different things, notice contrasts, notice differences in strength, quality, and texture.
Explore.
Stay with what you do sense. Allow the feelings that come through the awkwardness.

Can you be in this sense without needing to do anything?
After being in it, can you describe your experience?

Are there other senses activated as you explore this one?
Does this sensing take you somewhere else—to memory, feelings or other unrelated thoughts?

If you immediately shift to a more familiar sense, then be aware of your feelings. You may be avoiding an awkwardness or discomfort.
Spending time with the less-used sense stretches you.
You may have lots to learn from this perspective.

Do it now.

After you are finished sensing, pay attention.
How are you feeling now?
Can you describe some of the sensations you experienced?
Has your sensing stirred up memories or emotions?
Has anything changed in you from your explorations?
Describe everything you're aware of.

It may take some time to begin to express an unused sense with words and language, but it does get easier. Your description builds a bridge between those different parts of your being. By becoming receptive to an unused sense, you can open up a new richness and depth that you never even knew was there. You can enliven your other senses with new presence of mind and awareness. The immediate richness of your present experience will unfold into greater self-awareness.

Chapter 24

O you who love clear edges more than anything... watch the edges that blur.
Adrienne Rich

Conscious Description

New and often surprising experiences occur whenever we attend to the present. Each moment opens up into a rich flow of surprise and discovery. The better you can be present with your experience and describe it, the clearer your communication becomes with yourself and others. When your intention is to perceive something, to be open towards knowledge or an intuitive sense, what flows into you will be intuitive. All you need to do is attend to what is present. Start there and more will come.

Accurate description releases the energy behind the perception. So, it's helpful to be aware of the vocabulary you use. For example, take the word "membrane". What is the feeling that goes with this word for you? Take a moment and be with your sense of that word. Write down the word as you remember the feeling. That practice connects you with the experience of the word. The next time you encounter that feeling from inside, you will be more able to describe it accurately. You can also notice the way you describe things.

> *Once again, revisit your body focuses.*
> *Are you often using the same words?*

It's OK if you experience the same thing every time. But if your experience changes in some way, you may want to clarify and enlarge your descriptions. You don't have to worry about learning new words. All you have to do is pay attention to the differences you experience. As you pay attention, you will start to discriminate more.

If you use a word like "calm" at different times to describe your mood, then notice, were you actually feeling the same way each time? If not, then attend to the differences between those two feelings. Your description may then become "not quite calm" and might lead into "slightly agitated," "quiet," or "peaceful" as you stay with your feeling. Each word carries a different feeling. You can recognize when the word fits the feeling by the felt sense of a connection within you.

Learning to discriminate teaches you how to wait in unknowing. You have to be present in order to notice if your description is truly resonant with what you are experiencing. This keeps your conscious mind from stepping in and derailing your perceptual process with a label.

Timed Sensing

Here's a way you can build your vocabulary. This is a good exercise to do while you're engaged in some other activity, like reading, working, or talking with someone.

> *Get a kitchen timer or a stopwatch with an alarm.*
> *Set it for between 8 to 10 minutes.*
> *Pick a channel of perception such as your mental state,*
>   *emotions, or one of your senses.*
> *Describe what you are perceiving in that channel.*
>
> *Then continue doing whatever task you are doing.*
>
> *If you're moving, carry the timer with you.*

When the timer goes off, pause right at that moment and be aware what you are perceiving in the sense you've chosen.
Notice what is immediately there when you attend to it.
Open up briefly to the depth of that sense.
Describe it to yourself.

Do the words you use accurately communicate your perception?
If not, then spend a little more time with that perception.

Then reset your timer.
Return to your tasks until the next reminder.

You can do this process through the course of an entire day.
Each time you describe your sense, notice if you're using the same descriptors.
What you are sensing will be changing in some way.
Can your description match your changing experience?

You can begin this exercise while you're reading.

This exercise helps you build an awareness of the tremendous amount of change always flowing through your awareness. You will also increase your attentional flexibility. You will learn how to quickly shift from a conscious focus to a receptive, open state of mind and then back again to your conscious focus. For those wanting another effective tool for this timed awareness, I have produced a CD with relaxing water sounds and a chime for this purpose. Repeat this exercise with different senses, emotions or mental processes.

It takes conscious intent and a shift in your frame of mind to be more receptive to your subtle perceptions. Once you entertain the possibility that you can perceive something meaningful, then information may start to enter into your consciousness more easily. Your intuitive perceptions may not be as direct or familiar as your normal reasoning processes, but they can be allowed and strengthened.

> *Cerebrally, intuition is sometimes referred to as lateral thinking. But that is not a definition; it simply suggests that intuition, unlike logic, is not sequential and forward-moving; it moves sideways.*
> Daniel Cappon[9]

Dreambody Peripherals

Intuition may be first perceived as a force or a pressure pulling softly at the edge of your conscious focus. For instance, many people who are visually oriented report that images appear first in their peripheral vision. The first conscious recognition is of a brief sense of movement, a color, a shape or even a brief image at the edge of their visual field. The information is peripheral to consciousness as well as to vision and can appear in a similar way with any sense. When this happens our first response is to turn our attention directly towards the periphery. When we do this, the image instantly goes away. It's chased off by the power of focused awareness. Then our conscious mind says, "Oh, that was just my imagination."

> **The dreambody is the greater constellation of our self which is far more than just the physical body or the ego, but includes conscious and unconscious parts.**

The fleeting nature of peripherals is similar to having someone's name on the tip of your tongue. When you grasp for the name, it recedes. But when you let go of striving or reaching for something, it comes all by itself. It may take time, but it will come. Finding a way to allow peripherals into consciousness, without "chasing" them away is vital if you want to receive the information they contain. Peripheral intuitive information will appear spontaneously because the unconscious is already bringing it into our awareness. All we have to do is be patient and allow it to arrive.

The dreambody is another term that describes the unconscious part of us that is bringing us this information. Arnold Mindell uses this term and has written extensively on how to work with the dreambody as a personal practice, as a way to work with illness, and as a relationship technique. 24 The dreambody is the greater constellation of our self which is far more than just the physical body or the ego; it includes conscious and unconscious parts. You may experience your dream body as a dream image with an "energy" or emotional quality, a creative impulse to write, create, dance or sing. Your dreambody may manifest as a perception that defies logic, you might see auras, hear voices, sense contact or intention from another or even feel unexplained emotions. Unexplained sensations and even the physical manifestations of illness and disease may be expressions of the dreambody.

Consciously we are only aware of a small portion of our entire self. The rest of us is in the dreaming body. Attending to peripherals when they arise and paying attention to unexpected moods or sensations are ways to bring the dreambody more into consciousness. Mindell refers to an "ignition" that occurs when these "dreaming" signals are allowed into consciousness. Attending to them allows the meaning and intent behind them to become conscious and inform us.

When these intentions are strong enough, they force their way into our consciousness. We may feel back pain, hunger, or even experience a precognitive knowing. The same thing happens with a mother who intuitively senses her child's distress. The signal becomes so strong that it overrides her conscious focus. For most spontaneous intuitions, messages from the unconscious become too strong to ignore. Up until that moment, there were probably many other, more subtle signals that didn't get through.

Cultivating sensory awareness allows you to perceive your dreambody's smaller signals. A fleeting peripheral image can be allowed flow gently into the center of your vision. You stay in an open receptive state and you do not shift to narrow, objective focus when something nudges at your periphery. You still have conscious awareness, but it is relaxed and open. You encourage the unconscious to continue speaking.

You can experience that layering of inner and outer by keeping your eyes open now and bringing to mind the face of a

person you know well.
In your mind, visualize their face as you also see the book in front of you.
Shift back and forth between the inner visioning and the physical sensing.

With practice you can allow the inner image to have equal strength as the outer, and thus let a spontaneous image come from your unconscious. Bringing multiple sensations simultaneously into your awareness teaches attentional flexibility. Entering into your sensation, as with the eye massage, shifts you from objective focus into more immersed sensation.

Even if you don't pay attention, the unconscious will get its message through. Your unconscious might be giving you a message when you're walking down the sidewalk and you trip on a bump in the concrete. Your body is communicating to your conscious awareness. You can ignore it and keep walking or you can attend to it. Right then, you could open your focus a bit to allow these messages into your conscious awareness. When you do so, you will come more into your body and more into balance with your dreaming body.

For example, imagine that you are at a party and someone behind you touches you on the shoulder. In that moment of uncertainty, you could engage your inner awareness first. You could feel the touch and the subtler senses that go with it. If you stay present and allow the uncertainty of that moment, much more information will become available to you. You may notice how your body has an initial reaction to the touch. You might perceive a distinct physical response throughout your body. Then when you do turn, you are already connected to what you are perceiving through other channels. What you see will add to your awareness. Any time we reach out to touch someone with a hand, a word or a phone call, we are in communication from the first intention to make contact. You can sense the first, subtle levels of connection when you open to them.

Peripheral Practice

The following exercise is a simple way to practice building

your peripheral awareness. Read through the entire exercise first.

> *Sit at a table and place a piece of blank paper directly in front of you.*
> *Fasten the paper to the table with some tape.*
> *Draw a little "X" or another symbol in the center of the paper for you to focus on.*
> *Find a magazine you haven't read yet or haven't read recently.*
> *Set it on the table off to the side of your non-writing hand approximately one and a half to two feet from the center of the paper.*
>
> *Soften your gaze while you're focusing on the center of your paper.*
> *Allow your awareness to stay centered on that spot, but open up your peripheral awareness to what is all around you.*
> *Bring in an awareness of sounds or smells that are in the space with you.*
> *Sense the flow of your breathing.*
> *Let your breathing relax and smooth out a little.*
> *Then, in a soft, receptive frame of mind, open the magazine at a random place with your non-writing hand.*
> *Without shifting your focus, be aware what you perceive from the magazine.*
> *You may quickly recognize something—a color, a shape or even a particular object. That's OK.*
> *Close the magazine again with your non-writing hand, keeping your place with your finger.*
> *Write down what you perceived.*
> *Describe everything you experienced, even feelings or other non-visual senses.*
> *Sketch some of the elements you perceived.*
>
> *Look at what you drew on the paper and read what you wrote.*
> *Fill in any other information you are aware of that you haven't described yet.*
> *Close your eyes.*

> *Your inner vision or memory might fill in some of the empty areas.*
> *Stay with what you perceived, not what you think you saw.*
> *Be sure to put down any feeling responses.*
>
> *Do it now.*

When you're finished describing, open the magazine and look at what is on the page you chose. Then, compare your results. Pay attention to the discrepancies between what's in the magazine and what's on your paper. They may indicate places where your mind interpreted what you were perceiving. Be aware what triggered your mental response. Perhaps a color and shape combination reminded you of something, or perhaps you were feeling some discomfort and your "guessing" was an attempt to control. What you filled in may also be intuitive. You may have perceived a depth that isn't immediately obvious from your visual, conscious perception. Be open to that.

If your magazine has lots of recognizable images, of people, places or buildings, then you can bring in more discernment. What are the hand positions of the people? What are their facial expressions? Ask more questions when you're in your soft focus to bring in more detailed information. You can also move the magazine further away or closer in and notice how this affects your perception.

> *Repeat this exercise with the magazine in different positions.*
> *Experiment with both sides of your periphery as well as above and below center.*
> *Later, let the magazine close without saving your place.*
> *See if you can identify the image from your peripheral perceptions.*

Practicing this soft perception will open the door to dreambody information. This exercise also bridges to intuitive awareness. When you close your eyes, even subtler impressions may arrive in your consciousness. When intuitive peripheral perceptions appear, you can acknowledge them without knowing what they are.

You can allow these peripheral perceptions to resolve at their own pace. These more subtle perceptions are only unknown to your conscious mind. In the unconscious they are already clear. If you are perceiving a visual image, you may experience it moving from the side of your vision into the center and into focus. Sounds will become clearer and recognizable and will also move into the center of your awareness. Indistinct feelings will resolve into tangible senses that have meaning to you. These initial sensations may then flow into other senses, emotions, or thoughts at their own pace.

I had a peripheral experience at an archaeological site. As we were excavating, I was working with my trowel in one section of the grid, carefully scraping away dirt. I was focused on the spot I was clearing, keeping a careful eye open for artifacts, bits of stone, plant matter or other material. As I was scraping away dirt, I noticed a vague image out of the left corner of my eye. My first conscious awareness was of a blur of color. But I was barely even conscious of it. I was primarily focused on my digging. The image became clearer. A part of my awareness was drawn to it. In that moment of being drawn towards it, I was still focused on my digging, yet was also partially straddling another, more diffuse awareness.

I relaxed my focus on the ground where I was digging and relaxed my body. Then the image on the periphery clarified into a person's shoes standing right on the edge of the trench. Nothing strange. There were people walking all around the dig. But I saw leather moccasins, dark brown and black with small bits of color on them. The image was still off at the edge of my vision. It wasn't clear and in focus. I felt a surge of curiosity. My heart raced as I thought about what I was seeing. It was connected to what I was excavating, a prehistoric Native American site. In that rush of thinking I lost my equanimity and became much more excited. I wanted to "see" this person directly. I turned my head and looked in that direction. In that instant of turning, the image dissolved and I was left with just the feeling, a vibration, like a sound fading out of the air. I didn't perceive anything more, though the feeling stayed with me. I felt it was a person, a man watching us working.

Any time you experience a peripheral stimulus like the one I described, you have an indication that you are naturally shifting attentional styles and possibly brain wave states. We shift regularly into and out of different states, and these cycles are another way the unconscious guides us into health and balance. If a peripheral "suddenly" shows up on the screen of your conscious awareness, going with it may be a natural and healthy shifting of focus. It may be easier to go with that flow rather than holding on to your narrow conscious focus.

This shifting is similar to what happens when you're reading a book and you start to get sleepy. Even if you're really enjoying your book, the physical force of sleep starts to take away your conscious focus. That force is rising from your unconscious. If you're wrapped up in the story with your conscious mind, you can ignore this pull for awhile. But after a while it takes greater effort to stay focused. You may find yourself needing to reread a paragraph several times to register the information. You may slip into sleep in an instant when your focus wavers.

> When you're in narrow focused attention, messages from the periphery go entirely unnoticed.

Peripherals may also be information from the unconscious that's been put on hold. If we've spent time in a narrow conscious focus, then all the messages from other ways of knowing have been forced to wait, as if they're backed up in a cue. When they're important, they force their way into consciousness. If they are then still ignored, then they may not reach conscious awareness until we slip into sleep at night. Then everything that has been waiting is released into the dream state and processed there. The informing of our consciousness with these insights and perceptions still proceeds, although at an unconscious level.

When you're in narrow focused attention, messages from the periphery go entirely unnoticed. You can sense it in yourself if you focus all your awareness on this book. After a while you may forget about the needs of your body — having to go to the bathroom, needing to eat, or even needing to shift to a different position. After a while the peripheral begins to provide a stronger image or sense that pulls at your narrow-focused attention. Eventually it will intrude into your focus and you will notice.

A full-blown intuition of danger that calls us to full alertness or warns a mother of impending danger to her child is probably only the last of a series of ever-increasing messages from the unconscious. Most subconscious messages aren't deemed significant and are never consciously recognized.

Learning to allow the unconscious to lead means letting go of the conscious will and ego. Intuitive abilities are not as prevalent in our narrow focused culture. If our identity is based entirely on ego and individuality, then we will be threatened by these non-conscious forces. However, if we learn to value the parts of ourselves that are non-conscious and larger than our individual identity, then our sense of self becomes larger and more mindful.

Within the experience of now, you can experience a union with your deepest self outside any external associations or ego structures. This is the path of yoga or self-realization. Bringing your awareness to your most intimate thoughts and feelings, allows you to view them as something other than yourself. You have the opportunity to experience yourself as a deep flow of awareness. You can be present with the deepest parts of yourself. You can describe, be conscious and then release into a deeper and more present awareness and self-realization.

Deeper Body Focus

I'd like to introduce another variation of the body focus. Each time you do a body focus, your baseline becomes more familiar. Your body connection can become a meditation ritual, serving to focus your awareness and bring you into the present. It will provide a good starting point for your next experience, a more satisfying intuitive practice or a deeper meditation.

As you do this practice, you can heighten your sensitivity by moving your awareness into senses that you don't use as much. You can spend more time with your sense of smell, taste or touch opening the door to another kind of intelligence.

Read through this exercise. Then do it. For this extended body focus, I want you to focus on proprioception, the sensations that arise from within the body:

> Begin by attending to your general sense of the sensations within your body.
> You may only have a vague sense of health or sickness, high or low energy or even quietness.
> Can you imagine going a little deeper and feeling the body within its own sensations, attending to its language?
>
> Start at the lower part of your body.
> Feel your feet, your lower and upper legs.
> What qualities do they have?
> Notice what comes to your attention.
>
> Feel your pelvic region, your buttocks, genitals, and hips.
> Do you notice hot or cold spots, tension or pressure?
>
> Move up into your belly, and internal organs.
> Become aware of your back, spine, muscles, bones and nerves.
>
> Travel further up into your lungs and chest, front and back.
> Can you sense the beating of your heart?
> Do you feel energy in your upper body?
> Do you feel heat or pressure?
> How does your neck and head feel?
> Are there particular places on your head that you are more aware of?
> How about your skin?
>
> Is there a different quality that you can sense that's different from any discrete part?
>
> As you go into your body now, follow what you sense.
> Give yourself time to see what becomes stronger, what is waiting to be expressed and made conscious.

A physical sense may suddenly shift into another perception in a different channel.
You can be present and let your interior flow lead you.

You may also shift to a different sense spontaneously when you reach a wall, or an edge inside you, when a feeling becomes very strong and intense.
A feeling of itchy skin, as an example, can become quite overpowering.
Have you ever tried to allow it to subside on its own without scratching it?
Going with it may lead into a wholly different experience that carries meaning.
The itch may move into other channels and release in a different way.

You can explore body sensations that are disturbing, distracting or uncomfortable, and discover entirely new meanings behind them.
Let your dreambody unfold in your awareness.
Whatever grabs your attention is ready to unfold.
As your inner guide begins to lead, go with it.
Be aware.

Then communicate your perceptions.
Draw the feelings you are experiencing.
The moving hand and pen will facilitate the flow of your body/mind.
Words will also arise. Write them down as well.

Spend some time with your proprioception now.
Afterwards, make sure to reorient yourself in the present.
Are there other intentions that need expression?
Are your body, mind, heart or spirit needing some attention?
You can take care of yourself now.

Chapter 25

Deeper Questions

As you learn to use your intuition, the kinds of information you seek will evolve. You may have begun wanting to validate that intuition is real. When you accurately perceive a sound, a texture or a feeling, it can feel very exciting. As you continue, you may want more detail, accuracy, or complexity.

If you are already proficient in a particular line of work, your intuition may already be refined in that area, but you may want to expand your intuitive proficiency into other areas of your life. The kinds of information you can perceive is unlimited. If you can conceive of it, you can perceive it. You can intuitively perceive any level of understanding that interests or fascinates you. If there are any limits, they are only the ones you create for yourself.

You can approach any learning or exploration in the same way you would a tangible physical experience. You can check into each of your senses, change your orientation or perspective and even speed up or slow down what you are experiencing. You can perceive emotions, historical attributes, cultural and social information, and even subtle energetic properties. You can even bring in simple "Yes" or "No" questions about something you are sensing using your ideomotor responses. You can follow your curiosity wherever it takes you and expect a meaningful response.

You get a sense of how much information is accessible by paying attention to what you already know through normal means. Here's another exercise to heighten your sensitivity:

Pay attention to the physical space you are in now.
Then ask yourself some questions about this space and write down your responses.

What are the colors, textures, smells, and sounds here?
What is the temperature?
What is the shape and size of this space?
What is the purpose of this space?
What is this space called?
Are there energetic qualities in this space?
Are there activities happening here now?
Is anything changing in this present moment?
What is the history of this space?
What changes have occurred here?
What do you sense will be happening in the near future here?
What do you like about this space?
Do you experience a personal meaning in this space?

If there are people, animals or other creatures present with you, then you can ask yourself more questions.

How many people (creatures) are there?
How old are they?
How would you describe them?
What is their nationality or tribe?
What are their social connections?
Are they engaged in activities?
What emotions are they experiencing?
How healthy or unhealthy are they?
What do they do for a living?

Once you answered these questions, then ask yourself how you discovered each answer. For example, if you perceived a person's age, you may have used perceptions of body size or weight, hair color, clothing style, skin texture, or vocal quality. To determine the emotions they were feeling, you may have used similar observations as well as paying attention to the sensations you were experiencing.

If you repeat this process several times throughout the course of a day, you will quickly see just how much diverse information you process. If you want to know details about a person, your perception may begin with basic colors, sizes and textures. As you stay in the flow of perception and description, your intention will take you to what you want to know.

You can also start to use your creativity within your intuitive process. Say you're doing the intuitive exercise using the telephone. You allow whatever you're sensing to resolve and describe it. From these initial experiences, other questions come into your mind. You wonder if they will be sitting or standing. As the question flows through your mind, you relax and allow perceptions to come. You can follow your intent as it manifests and allow the answers to come.

If you're open to receiving spontaneous information, it may come out of the blue. For example, you're having lunch with a friend and you recognize a shift in your physical energy and a new clarity in your thinking. Rather than discounting it, you can ask yourself, "Is this important?" If you sense it is, then you might ask, "How is this important?" If there is more meaning, it will unfold as you pay attention. Your unconscious will lead you with elegant guidance. All you have to do is pay attention. When you don't know what you need, your unconscious will lead you along into an experience that is just right for you. Any time you don't know the meaning of something you're experiencing, you can ask:

"Is there anything that needs to be done now?"
Then relax and wait for an answer.

The Flow of the Space

By asking yourself first, you validate a deep part of your being. You will be led into a deeper trust not only of yourself, but of the entire universe. Remember, what is happening right now is already a response to your deepest intentions. You can love yourself more in this very moment. You can enjoy the nature of your experience as you experience it.

The next time you're at the beach, driving through a new neighborhood, in a shopping mall, or in any new place, you can use the environment to increase your awareness. As children we did this naturally. We would explore and be curious. Nothing was off limits.

In a natural environment, you have the benefit of rich sensory experiences, which your body is designed to love. You can look for rocks and fossils, plants, wildlife, land forms and geology, human artifacts, and even personal energetic changes. You can use the variety of natural phenomena to develop your attentional flexibility. When you arrive in a new place, you can start looking for interesting rocks. Start to pay attention to plants as well, or flowers. While you're engaged, listen for bird song or other sounds. You can still be interested in the rocks and other perceptions can be allowed. You can attend to the way your body responds to the space. You can intentionally expand in an open focus to let the interplay of all your senses inform you.

You can allow your awareness to flow from one point of focus to the next—shifting from an interesting rock, to the sound of a bird, to a memory, or to the smell of a breeze. The separation between inner and outer lessens and your experience of yourself begins to merge with a meaningful landscape. You begin to sense the quality and character of the space, and perhaps more importantly, a quality that is within you.

How you experience yourself in any space is connected to a personal question or a feeling you've been carrying with you. The dreaming energies of your unconscious and higher consciousness come through as a combination of inner sensations and outer experiences. Even during a walk along the seashore, collecting shells or looking for birds, deeper intentions will surface. Invite that sense the next time you venture into a new area. Exercise your capacity to expand your deeper being as you connect with the universe.

Chapter 26

Joan of Arc: I hear voices telling me what to do. They come from God.
Robert: They come from your imagination.
Joan of Arc: Of course. That is how the message of God comes to us.
- George Bernard Shaw

Natural Consciousness

Each full sensory moment opens up a connection to the vitality of the objective world. We may have a different felt sense that occurs when we immerse our awareness in a rock compared to our sensing of an animal or another human. When we stop objectifying what we are experiencing, we move into relationship with it.

Some form of consciousness resides in all matter, inside everything we experience. Granted, the consciousness in a rock may not be the same form of consciousness we experience. Yet our consciousness is intimately connected with the same physical elements, the molecules and compounds that are in our bodies. Through respiration, sensing, eating and digesting, we are constantly intermingling with the physical. What is in us mirrors our environment and vice versa.

We can utilize every object of our perception for reflection, mirroring and intuitive questing. When we open to our innate sensual experience, the entire world becomes a mirror for our inner landscape and the spiritual connection we have to it. We are conversely a mirror for the consciousness of the world; it is reflected in us.

The consciousness embedded in all "reality" is a major component of animism and shamanistic thinking. The world, including all the other forms of consciousness and being, is not separate from us as the materialistic, scientific paradigm has taught us to believe. You tap into this larger consciousness in the immediacy of your sensory experience, every time you pay attention and remain open to what you perceive. The largeness of the universe is not out there or somewhere else. It is inside you now.

> *What are you sensing now?*
> *How is the physical sensation you are perceiving different than the thought that passes through your mind or the emotion that arises inside you?*
> *Imagine that what you perceive as occurring outside you is an intimate part of your core self.*
> *Imagine that what you are perceiving outside of you is a reflection of an inner part of your self.*

The external world may be revealing to you a part of yourself that you've lost touch with, one that lies outside your conscious self. A sound you hear may be the manifestation of a different part of you much the same way your stomach growls to tell you that you're hungry. If you hear a sound, then it is already part of you, in your experience. If you embrace the idea of consciousness everywhere, then the physical object that created the sound is in some way resonating with your inner intent. Anything that thrums your mind/body system is resonant with a deeper part of you.

You can "decode" these incoming messages by letting yourself experience them fully. Your experience may not make sense in a rational way. You may not even be able to put words to what you perceive. Yet as you validate your intangible experiences, you strengthen your connection to the larger you. As you open to the potential meaningfulness of your sensory experience, your experience of yourself becomes larger. You can immerse yourself into the loving embrace of a larger "body" of being.

Falling in Love

In India this immersion is called Bhakti. It is one of the main yogas, or paths, leading to spiritual awareness. Bhakti is the path of devotion. Bhakti is commonly thought of as a devotion to a form or a God, but, from the sensory perspective, it could be the immersion in anything with openness and love. You can be devoted to what is present now in your awareness. Devotion is loving immersion. It is another manifestation of trance where the focus removes separation. Sri Ramana Maharshi says Bhakti is the absence of thoughts and the immersion of the self into God. [21]

Even a simple sensory moment can lead you into a deeply profound awareness. You experience this shift in meaning, and the mundane becomes sacred. The essence of this sacred feeling lies outside any particular belief system about God or spirit. It is the awareness of being. You can experience yourself intimately connected with the entire universe and fall in love with your living present.

> You can be devoted to what is present now in your awareness. Devotion is loving immersion. It is another manifestation of trance, where the focus removes separation.

I've had a deeply profound experience of immersion in the world of sensory experience. In 1986 I spent some time at an ashram in India. During that period, I was repeating the mantra "Soham" as much as I could. This Sanskrit word means "I am that" or "That I am." The mantra appealed to me intellectually. Also, I understood this mantra had been used by meditators for millennia. I wanted the extra energy of that extra morphogenic field.

I would say the "so" sound inside my head on the inhale and the "ham" on the exhale. It can be done either way. The sounds would blend together at the shifting point of the breath, becoming a continuous flow of awareness. I had this mantra in my breath as much as I could as I went about the events of the day. Other thoughts and feelings would come and pass through this focus, and I allowed myself to go with them. I practiced allowing each "that" I focused on to also be part of the "I am" of myself.

One afternoon, sitting in the shade by myself, listening to the crows, I experienced a profound shift in consciousness. The best I can describe it is that I became the mantra. I became "I am that." The rising and falling of that word synchronized with my breathing in an effortless flow. It spread out and merged with my entire awareness. The sounds of the crows were inside that effortless flow. I experienced no separation. It was the same with the buildings across the courtyard, the sand, the concrete, the trees, and even the crows themselves. Everything was pulsing, alive and vibrant, within the flow of this "I am." I was not separate from any of it. I was inside it and alive with it.

In that flow, time stopped. I don't know how long it lasted, only that at some point, perhaps only a few moments later, I began thinking again. My awareness switched back to subject and object. I was "me" again feeling euphoric, dazed and bewildered.

> This present moment is a doorway leading out of ego into a profound connection with spirit.

My memory of this experience is a shadow of the actual experience but it still holds power for me. When I remember it now, I still can still revivify some of the original experience. It reminds me how it is possible to experience everything as intimately connected to my sense of self. The strongest memory I have of this experience is the felt sense of it. I felt a tremendous joy and freedom. I believe I had an experience of immersed awareness as symbolized in the perception figure on page 127.

This kind of experience is one of the major goals of meditation. The fullness of being unfolds automatically when the narrow focus of the ego is suspended. You don't have to be practicing

Bhakti or Mantra yoga to have a similar experience, although having a practice is helpful. The same connection is always occurring within us, through the intimacy of the present moment. This present moment is a doorway leading out of ego into a profound connection with spirit. It can be tapped into, explored and allowed to unfold in a meaningful way.

With a sensory awareness practice you learn to alternate between these two poles. Immersion leads to awareness and description which moves back into the next immersed moment. Judging one state as better than the other sets up a duality. Think of both as equally valuable. Relaxing into your flow, you open the door to a fully conscious immersion—a peak experience—and the following integration of that experience when you come back out. Rumi puts the paradox another way:

> *One group walks toward the fire, into the fire,*
> *another toward sweet flowing water.*
> *No one knows which are blessed and which not.*
> *Whoever walks into the fire appears suddenly in the stream.*
> *A head goes under on the water surface,*
> *that head pokes out of the fire.*
> *Most people guard against going into the fire,*
> *and so end up in it.*
> *- Translations of Rumi by Coleman Barks with John Moyne* [3]

The fire represents the path that seems the hardest to you or the one you struggle with. You may feel you need to work to attain your goal and thus enter the fire, or you may take the easier way into your water. Either way, you come out on the other side. If you have an affinity for immersion or bhakti, you will at some point move outwards again, back into objectivity. This is a natural way of integrating your experience. When the shift to objectivity brings you back from an immersed, intuitive experience, it allows you to communicate what you're experiencing and extend it out back to the world.

We tend to seek a sense that we enjoy, and avoid ones we

don't. If you're on the fire path, then you avoid the experiences that are comfortable. You are attached to the uncomfortable. To whatever degree we cling to or avoid something we perceive as good, we suffer when it starts to change. This will happen any time the thing we hold onto is something other than the center of our being, or the "I am."

The "I am" is a flow or a process of evolving spirit. When you shift from being to knowing or back again, you go outside of yourself, outside your comfort zone. It can happen when you're experiencing a table, an apple, or a mantra. Both paths of immersion and objectivity flow in and out of each other, the same way your breath flows in and out. Neither is necessarily better or worse.

This kind of flexibility can be unintentionally trained out of you if you use an intuitive or spiritual discipline that is too narrowly focused. If the techniques you practice are very controlled, you can lose the ability to experience the full range of your being. Going too far into the flow, following a 'higher power,' can be equally detrimental if you lose your ability to make your own choices and integrate what you learn. Ask yourself:

> *What is the purpose of being in this situation, reading this material or having this experience?*
> *Can you invite an intelligence that goes beyond the boundaries of your conscious intent?*

Each exercise you do can serve your entire self, rather than just your conscious ego. If you want to experience higher or more realized consciousness, that's fine, but don't let your ego lead the way. Maintaining a connection to your deeper self while engaging in the world is the difference between knowing the practice and living it. The practical side of balancing comes when you combine your intuitive, spiritual exploration with your practical, day to day needs. You can leave openings in your life for the transpersonal, but still attend to your personal concerns.

Personal Intuition Questions

Directing intuition towards personal matters can be difficult.

When you're looking at your choices, you have conscious thoughts about them and preferences. What you know and think with your conscious mind tends to get in the way of your subtler, intuitive senses. The following exercise is designed to get your conscious mind out of the way. Read through the entire exercise before starting.

Personal intuition questions:
1 - *Choose three different questions or topics you want more information on. Each should be on a different subject. One should be more emotionally important, one not, and the third, somewhere in between. Try to come up with questions where you are seeking to know information about something, not just a "yes" or "no" response. For example, if you wanted to know if you should fly somewhere, you could ask what the trip will be like going there, rather than if you should or shouldn't go. It's easier to get information about an experience. After you have that information you can consciously decide if you should go or not.*
2 - *Write each question at the top of a blank sheet of paper and fold it three or four times, so the text is hidden inside. Fold each paper the same way.*
3 - *Shuffle the three folded papers.*
4 - *Put them into three blank envelopes and seal them.*
5 - *Shuffle the three envelopes.*
6 - *Set them aside for several hours or perhaps an entire day. Then shuffle them again. You can repeat the shuffling as many times as you need to be sure you have no way of knowing which envelope contains which question. You can even allow yourself to forget your questions.*
7 - *When you're ready to start, number the envelopes. Take one envelope and a sheet of paper and write the envelope number on the sheet. Do whatever you need to do to put yourself into a receptive, intuitive frame of mind. Then do your intuitive process to perceive information about the question. The question in the envelope is your target.*

As with all exercises, accept any kind of information you perceive. Anything that happens to you is in some way a response to the target. Report everything you experience by drawing or describing. If you think you are answering one particular question, make a note of it.
What makes you think that? Then let it go, and go back to your direct perceptions. Make sure and describe everything you are experiencing, even your thoughts, frustrations, and distractions that you know are not related to the target.

8 - *When you've done as much as you want to do, set that one envelope aside. Fold the sheet of paper in half with the text inside and set it aside. Don't open your envelope yet.*

9 - *Repeat steps #7 and #8 with the other two envelopes. It's a good idea to take a break and do something else in between each envelope. You may even do one each day, over a period of three days.*

10 - *Once you've done all your envelopes, you can go further if you'd like, if you are patient enough. To deepen your intuitive connection before getting feedback, you can do step #11. If you're ready for your feedback skip to step #12.*

11 - *Set the three sheets with your written information aside. Turn the three envelopes upside down so you can't see the numbers. Shuffle them up a time or two. Come back later and shuffle them again. Then when you're ready label the back side of the envelopes A, B, and C. Pick one envelope and work it again using steps #7 and #8. Put the letter you're working on your new sheet of paper. When you're done, set it and the envelope aside without looking at the number on the other side envelope.*
Repeat this process for the other two envelopes, taking time to rest in between each one. Make sure you don't look at the numbers. This second step allows you a fresh, and possibly different, perspective for each of your questions. Not seeing the numbers allows you to separate from your first sessions with each envelope and get a better overall response.

12 - *When you're ready for feedback, compile all your results for each number and letter. Open the envelope and*

reread your question. Then, when you read your feedback, remember to pay attention to your feelings. If something you wrote resonates with you in some way, make a note of it. You may even describe that sense to help clarify what you are experiencing as you read. What you experience while you are reading is part of the process. You may get a sense how your responses relate to your question. At the very least you will get a different perspective.

This process can help you explore questions that are emotionally loaded. For example, if you have a health issue on your mind, make it the focus of one of your questions. You can frame your question in different ways. One way would be to look at your progress. Your question could be, "What action do I need to take now regarding the (whatever the issue is)?" You could also focus on information gathering. You could ask, "What is causing the sensation in my (your body part)?" or "What information would be helpful in my healing?"

Then be sure to also choose other questions that are not as emotionally loaded. That way you'll be able to detach more and allow new information into your awareness. You can also bring this exploration into a group intuitive process as I will explain. Getting different, fresh perspectives can provide valuable insight into a long-term or chronic problem.

Are there some questions you would like to explore?

Expanding to Groups

As I've discussed intuition throughout this book, the focus has been on individual awareness. But, we must remember, even in our private process, intuition is about communication. Intuition is a quality of consciousness that manifests in relationship, internal or external. It is a translation of the energy of one state of consciousness into another one. The only way we recognize intuition is through the perspective of our conscious personality. Outside of our conscious self, in experiences that we have as pure consciousness, intuitive knowing and all of its connections are normal qualities of that state of being.

What we receive through intuition is given its meaning because of the way it comes through us. We may alter our behavior and our relationships, we don't say something or we do, or we change what we were going to do. Internal intuitions change the way we are within ourselves. The meaningfulness of intuition only comes in relationship. When intuition becomes activated and explored, it will inevitably extend into relationships. Our consciousness will be extended out into the physical world.

Find a group of like-minded friends to share in your intuitive exploration. They will keep you grounded. Start talking, sharing insights, practicing together, and helping each other. Keep the group diverse. You can even invite people who don't know each other. By that choice the experiences and information gained in the group will be more grounded in shared reality. Variety in personality, history, and age will also bring in different belief systems. Everyone will grow beyond their personal limitations.

> Trusting yourself in group work is an extension of the self-trust and validation you gain with your private practice. The feedback and validation you receive in a group can be very empowering.

As soon as you start working with a group, other doors will start to open. All the personal experiences begin to take on a group dynamic. You will notice an even greater degree of unconscious guidance. One person's experience may trigger another's insight or understanding. Each person's success serves as confirmation to others as well as stronger validation for the person experiencing. Being intuitive with other people makes the phenomena more real.

A group working together and exploring intuition can begin to address specific questions with its group mind. As a group, you can work on one person's personal interest, a shared question, or even a larger community issue. One person can write down a personal question. Then the others can respond without knowing the question. (Use the personal intuition questions exercise on the previous pgaes.) You can even practice spontaneous responses to spoken questions. Each member of the group trusting whatever comes first.

Groups working the same target will produce similar information more likely to be accurate or meaningful to the whole group. Pieces of information that aren't resonant with others are still meaningful. Such information may be strictly personal to the individual.

One person may get one piece of information that no one else perceives. If she trusts herself, she will still share it with the group. As an individual working in a group intuitive process, you don't know what parts of your intuitive process are personal and what parts are communal. Thus it's important to speak and express whatever you experience, especially when you sense your inner movement guiding or directing you. What you think is personal may be, but it may also have meaning to someone else in the group. Trusting yourself in group work is an extension of the self-trust and validation you gain with your private practice. The feedback and validation you receive in a group can be very empowering.

Also, with group work comes a whole different level of personal manifestation, as expressed in relationship. The group expands the non-physical qualities of the intuitive experience into a shared group experience. You will have an extension of the personal joy that is felt when the conscious mind lets go. That other power, the ally, comes into experience.

With a group, this power becomes much stronger, more perceptible, and transformative. The intent of a group working with intuition becomes a flow of greater intent that goes far beyond individual intentions. When you make the focus of the group service to something larger, your group exploration can take on new exciting dimensions. The group is not limited to what can be controlled and directed by the conscious mind. A group of intuitives working together could conceivably transform how we manifest change. Physical healing, scientific discovery, and even social transformation become possibilities.

Pause...

You can remember and revisit things you enjoy.

Body Markers and Anchors - You can pay attention to changes that occur in your body. They can lead your consciousness. You can use your body changes consciously. You can remember the feeling and touch yourself in a particular way to engage your consciousness.

Psychometry - Use the sense of touch as a doorway into intuition. Use stones, money or other personal objects as entry points into your intuitive connection.

Palming and Massage - Touch yourself more. Put your hands over your eyes to calm your whole being. Move into the sense of touch on your body to calm yourself, balance your energies and give yourself joy.

Timer - Use a timer to build vocabulary and sensory awareness.

Open Focus - Practice perceiving space. Open your awareness to include multiple channels of perception. Use natural environments and your fascination to perceive the connection between yourself and the rest of the natural world.

Personal Intuition Questions - Use your intuition for practical questions. Do you have a health issue, a relationship or financial question, or want to explore a community question?

Chapter 27

Living Intuition

No matter how you plan to continue exploring your intuitive awareness, you can be present with yourself now. Your next insight begins this moment. With intent, you can generate the sensitivity and openness to allow the presence of the "visitor" to flow into your life. Remember that it really isn't the specific intuitive or awareness techniques that are important. Learning how to be fully present with yourself is what's meaningful. Practicing intuition may in the end bring you more the joy of being present, alive and aware. These are worthy goals.

So, as you proceed, make time to be present with yourself. Each sensing, each exploration, and each extension of intention and letting go can be a joyful discovery of yourself. You can have very concrete intuitive experiences. You can allow yourself unstructured and introspective time as well.

You can always start by attending to what is already happening. Do the structure of a body focus if you like where it takes you. Become aware of the openings already inside you. You can be responsive to the powerful movements of your deeper self as they arise. They are all openings for growth and expansion. You can also explore your darker dreaming parts with care and tenderness. Your distractions, your difficulties, your struggle and even your pain are also valuable doorways into yourself.

Each time you experience a shift in your body or a change in your awareness you may ask yourself, "What does this mean?" or "What is this telling me?" Pay attention and wait for an answer. If there is something you want to know, express that intent clearly and then let it go. Be receptive to whatever comes into you. Enjoy the flow of your being in formation. Then describe what you're experiencing, if only to yourself. Communicate what you perceive and stay in your flow of becoming.

You can be more and more receptive to the greater intentions of your being—your spiritual side, your emotional side, even your connection to the more-than-human world. You can immerse your self into your experience and become more alive. You can also let go of constant doing and allow the emptiness of your deepest self guide you.

The techniques you've explored in this book can help you deepen your personal, spiritual practice. As you learn to trust yourself more, you can release old fears and limiting beliefs. You can use your full awareness to move into community, to be respectful and responsive to others and to engage in open dialogue with other beliefs and views of reality. You will transform from the inside out. You will heal yourself and others around you.

Read through your answers to the belief questionnaire you filled out on page 69. Notice any changes. How would you answer differently now? Any differences you see in your beliefs will reveal your ever-changing self. Each small change opens the door for larger transformation.

Can you imagine larger changes?
Can you allow them to manifest?

You can experience being connected in an intimate way to everything that exists in your life. With respect, attention and love, you can care for and heal yourself and your world. When you finish this book and move into the next activity of your life, your inner connection will guide you. As you become more receptive, your intuition will become stronger. You can enter into each moment with the full presence of your being.

I remember listening to a talk Ram Dass gave some time before the year 2000. He was asked what he was planning to do if there was a major disaster of some kind as we crossed into the next millennium. He basically said if something happened, he would quiet his mind, open his heart and do the best he could to relieve the suffering of those around him. When asked what he would do if nothing happened, he gave the same answer—quiet his mind, open his heart, and do the best he could to relieve the suffering of those around him. To me that is congruence. You can become a guest house, a place of waiting and receptivity, a place of appreciation, validation, and joy. You can become a vital person using your higher power.

I recognize I am now living more fully in the present than I ever have. I fully expect my awakening to continue. I welcome the joyful discovery as well as the letting go and grief for what I have left. I appreciate all the conscious and unconscious forces that moved me to this point. These forces include all the reflections of consciousness and spirit flowing through me—plants and animals, rocks and trees, the wind and the sun, my history and my possible futures. Remember the picture at the beginning of the book on page 25? The place in that photo is a significant space for me; it is part of what moved me along my path. I feel an energy there that is part of my personal unfoldment. What do you sense there?

You can use your intuition, and trust it.

As you proceed from this moment, the wholeness of your being will guide you with an elegance far beyond the capacities of your conscious mind. As the conversation continues with all the parts of your being, you become the crystallization of your greater intent. You can become the full dancing beauty of a human being.

What are you experiencing now?
Is there a deeper, loving part of you guiding you towards your next experience?
You can follow your self.

Appendix A
Targets for Intuitive Practice

If you have access to the internet, the www.rvtargets.com web site has an abundant supply of practice targets. To use this site, you simply log in, then request a new target. You will receive a target number such as "RVG1262470201". Write down your number and use it at your leisure, whenever you're ready to practice your intuitive exercise. Speak or write the number to yourself when you're ready, and your unconscious will know where to go.

When you're finished and you want feedback, return to the web site, login again, and click on the link to receive feedback. You will then have the option to enter your perceptions or just view the target photo. Remember the photo is just the visual part of the feedback. You may have received much more information about the target such as smell, touch, taste, emotion or more complex understandings. Be sure to follow the intuitive process I outlined on pages 142-144 to connect with the feedback before you evaluate your results.

If you don't have internet access, you can create your own pool of practice targets. You can do this yourself, or have a friend do it for you. To begin, you will need a set of identical envelopes. Large manilla envelopes for mailing work well because you can use standard sized sheets of paper for your targets without needing to fold them. However, any envelopes will work as long as they're identical.

Into the envelopes you will put photos and written descriptions of your targets. The photos from National Geographic magazine work well for targets, as do old photo calendars, travel brochures and even newspapers. What you're looking for are photos of objects, activities, people, or events that are interesting. Also, as you're beginning it's good to use photos that aren't too complex. Pictures that are primarily of one object, activity or living thing work well. It is also helpful if your target has multiple senses. For example a picture of a horse in a barn would be good because it has images, smells, sounds, textures, shapes and the energy of a living being, lots of information for you to perceive.

Be sure to include many different kinds of targets. You don't want all animals for example. Include buildings, landscapes, natural and man-made places, calm, serene places as well as busy ones. When you include targets with people in them, be sure to include the whole range of emotion and activity. All of this variety will ensure that you don't know what to expect when you intend to perceive an individual target. Your conscious mind will have to relax and allow your unconscious to guide you to the information.

Once you have your targets collected, trim off any unwanted pictures or information. Glue the pictures onto blank white sheets of paper. This way, you will not see the back sides of the pictures which contain irrelevant information. You will only get feedback on the target you've selected. Then write a very short description of your target below the picture. For example, for the photo of the horse I mentioned, I would write, "Horse in Barn". This brief description serves to focus the intention of what you're wanting to perceive, which will help your accuracy as you become more skilled.

The last step in creating each target is to insert each target photo into its own envelope and seal it. You may even include a blank page on top of your colored photos to insure no image is visible through the envelope. If you're creating the targets for yourself then you're finished. However, if someone else is creating targets for you, they can add a number to the target description, such as "0001 - Horse in Barn". Then, they would then also write that number on the outside of the envelope. Create at least twenty of these practice targets, seal them, and set them aside for a few days.

You can use your targets as part of your own practice or working with the exercises in this book. If you've created your own target pool, choose one target to use for your exercise and set it with you wherever you're sitting. When it comes time to perceive, tell yourself, "I want to perceive the target in this envelope." If it has a number, you could say, "I want to perceive target (number)."

Have fun!

Appendix B - Websites

Belleruth Naparstek - belleruthnaparstek.com
  Belleruth's site has many resources on health, healing and intuition. Her book, <u>Your Sixth Sense</u>, is a great resource for learning practical intuition.
Boundary Institute - www.gotpsi.org/bi/gotpsi.htm
  This is the site where Dean Radin is conducting his on-line psychic testing. There are three tests here you can participate in with feedback on your success. You can get immediate feedback on your performance.
Charles Tart - http://www.paradigm-sys.com/
  This page has links to Tart's activities, writings and research. A wonderful resources of 50 years of consciousness research.
International Remote Viewing Association - www.irva.org
  This site has information on the Association and general information on Remote Viewing practices and protocols. It also has links to other RV sites and the RV conference site.
Jeffrey Mishlove - http://www.williamjames.com/BlogIndex.htm
  This site is the index of Mishlove's blog. He has spent many years researching intuition and consciousness.
Lyn Buchanan's test targets - www.crviewer.com/TARGETS/TargetIndex.asp

> Lyn Buchanan's site has a list of test targets that you can work with.

Marty Rosenblat - Physics Intuition Applications - www.p-i-a.com
> Marty does a lot of work with associative remote viewing and prediction.

Open Focus - http://openfocus.com/
> This is the website for Les Fehmi. It includes some nice practice exercises for developing an open focus state.

Pam Coronado - www.pamcoronado.com
> Pam trained with Alan Vaughn and Bevy Jeagers and has worked since 1996 in psychic criminal work. Her book, <u>Psychic Basic Training</u> is a great resource.

Paul Smith - Remote Viewing Instructional Services - rviewer.com/index.html
> This site has many resources, training options and examples of the controlled remote viewing methodology.

Penney Peirce - www.penneypeirce.com/library.htm
> Penney is an intuitive empath, speaker and a trainer. Her library page has some great resources for intuitives.

Psi Arcade - www.psiarcade.com/
> Sponsored by the Institute of Noetic Sciences

RV targets on-line - www.rvtargets.com/
> A great resource of on-line targets with feedback. You can log-in, get a coordinate, do your session at your leisure, then get feedback.

Stephan Schwartz - www.stephanaschwartz.com
> Articles on remote viewing and archaeology, as well as references to work with George McMullen.

Sensory Awareness Foundation - http://www.sensoryawareness.org/
> This website presents the ongoing work in sensory awareness which was pioneered by Charlotte Selver.

Appendix C - Glossary

Analytical Overlay (AOL) - Conscious mental interference and/or analysis of intuitive information. Usually interferes with intuitive process and creates noise.

Baseline - The average or normal framework within which we experience the world and ourselves. A constellation of certain senses, attitudes and behaviors that make up our selves as we participate with the world.

Body focus - A sensory awareness exercise for bringing conscious attention to the phenomena present in awareness. A process of checking into each of the physical senses, the quality of mind and the emotions. This checking in allows a freeing up of energy associated with unrecognized information registering in the psyche. This energy can then be channelled by conscious intention, or allowed to flow guided by the dreambody.

Channel - An identifiable path through which information passes between the conscious and the unconscious or between the self and the non-self. A channel includes the physical senses, inner senses, emotions, thoughts, physical and non-physical bodies.

Clear Intent - A state of being where conscious and unconscious intentions are resonant and acting together, where awareness of the present is balanced with intentions towards the future and the past.

Dialogue - a stream of meaning flowing through and around the subject and object. Dialogue is more about process than content. The quality of your engagement informs you.

Fascination - The state of being intensely interested or attracted. A resonance between an inner aspect of ourselves and an externally perceived phenomena. Enjoy it, and be aware you are also fascinated and attracted to something in yourself.

Hypnagogic - Of or relating to the state of drowsiness preceding sleep. Also relating to the phenomena associated with this state.

Hypnopompic - Of or relating to the state of drowsiness after sleep.

Ideomotor - Of or relating to an unconscious or involuntary bodily movement made in response to a thought or an idea rather than to a sensory stimulus.

Intuition - An awareness, understanding or perception that enters conscious awareness by means other than normal conscious mental processing or the use of the physical senses.

Noise - Information in an intuitive process that has no relevance or meaning to the target.

Portal - An entrance or a means of entrance. En - trance. That which can take you in.

Proprioception - The unconscious perception of movement and spatial orientation arising from stimuli within the body itself.

Psychometry - An intuitive technique that uses physical objects as the entry point or catalyst for receiving information.

Remote Viewing - A protocol that uses intuition in a structured way to access information that is not accessible through normal sensing or cognitive means.

Spontaneous - 1. Happening or arising without apparent external cause; self-generated. 2. Arising from a natural inclination or impulse and not from external incitement or constraint. 4. Growing without cultivation or human labor; indigenous.

Appendix D - Bibliography

1 Abram, David. *The Spell of the Sensuous.* New York: Vintage Publishing, 1997.
2 Baars, Bernard. *In the Theater of Consciousness.* New York: Oxford University Press, 2001.
3 Barks, Coleman and Moyne, John. *The Essential Rumi.* San Francisco: Harper, 1995.
4 Barks, Coleman and Moyne, John. *We Are Three.* Athens, Georgia: Maypop Books, 1988.
5 Bower, Bruce. "The Mental Butler Did It". *Science News*, Vol. 156, Pg. 280-82, Oct. 30 1999. Society for Science and the Public.
6 Bower, Bruce, "Snooze Power", *Science News*, Vol. 161, Pg. 341, June 1, 2002. Society for Science and the Public.
7 Brooks, David, "The Creative Moment", *Southerly*, Autumn 1998 v58, Pg. 31(3). The Australia Council.
8 Campbell, Joseph. From the video, *Mythos Vol. 1.* Acacia.
9 Cappon, Daniel, "The Anatomy of Intuition", *Psychology Today,* May-June 1993 v26 n3, Pg. 40(9). Sussex Publishers LLC.
10 Carse, James. *Finite and Infinite Games.* New York: Ballantine Books, 1987.
11 Coats, Callum. *Living Energies.* California: Gateway, 2002.
12 De Quincey, Christian. *Radical Nature.* Vermont: Invisible Cities Press LLC, 2002.

13 Donoso, Steve. "In the power of presence, an interview with Ehkart Tolle". *Noetic Sciences Review*, Mar-May 2003. California: Institute of Noetic Sciences.
14 Edwards, Betty. *Drawing on the Right Side of the Brain*. California: Tarcher, 1979.
15 Erickson, Milton and Rossi, Ernest. *Experiencing Hypnosis*. New York: Irvington Publishers, 1981.
16 Fehmi, Lester and Robbins. *Open Focus Brain: Harnessing the Power of Attention to Heal Mind and Body*. California: Trumpeter, 2008.
17 Harmin, Willis. Interview in *Business Ethics*, March-April 1992. New York: New Mountain Media.
18 Huxley, Aldous, *The Art of Seeing*. New York: Harper, 1942.
19 Isenman, Lois. "Toward an understanding of intuition and its importance in scientific endeavor". *Perspectives in Biology and Medicine*, Spring 1997 v40 n3, p395(9). Maryland: The Johns Hopkins University Press.
20 Jaegers, Beverly. *Personal communication*. November, 2000.
21 Maharshi, Sri Ramana. *Talks with Sri Ramana Maharshi*. Ottowa: Laurier Books Ltd., 1994.
22 Mavromatis, Andreas. *Hypnagogia: the Unique State of Consciousness Between Waking and Sleep*. New York: Routledge, 1987.
23 McMullen, George. *One White Crow*. Charlottesville: Hampton Roads Publishing Company, 1995.
24 Mindell, Arnold. *Dreambody: The Body's Role in Revealing the Self*. Portland: Lao Tse Press, 1998.
25 Mishlove, Jeffery. *Psi development systems*. North Carolina: McFarland & Co Inc., 1984.
26 Pierce, Penny. *The Intuitive Way: A Guide to living from Inner Wisdom*. Hillsboro: Beyond Words, 2009.
27 Roberts, Jane. *The Education of Oversoul Seven*. United Kingdom: Pocket, 1987
28 Schwartz, Stephen. *The Alexandria Project*. Nebraska: IUniverse, 2001.
29 Selver, Charlott. *Learning Through Sensing*. This article is based on two of the published tapes from Charlotte Selver's

11-14-77 class at Green Gulch Farm and 7-31-80 class on Monhegan Island. www. sensoryawareness.org, 2008.
30 Selver, Charlotte and Brooks, Charles. "Report on work in sensory awareness and total functioning", From Otto, Herbert A., Ph. D., *Explorations in Human Potentialities.* Illinois: Charles C. Thomas, 1966.
31 Tart, Charles. "Acknowledging and Dealing With the Fear of Psi". *Journal of the American Society for Psychical Research.* New York: American Society for Psychical Research, 1984.
32 Ventura, Michael. "Looking Quickly To The Side: The Other World of Psychic Phenomena." *Utne Reader,* Sept-Oct, 1989. Topeka: Ogden Publications.
33 Watson, Lyall. *The Nature of Things: The Secret Life of Inanimate Objects.* Vermont: Destiny Books, 1992.
34 White, Rhea. "A Comparison of Old and New Methods of Response to Targets in ESP Experiments". *The Journal of the American Society for Psychical Research,* Volume 58, January, 1964, no. 1. New York.

Index

A

affirmation 201
allowing 134, 263
alpha frequencies 32
altered states 49
analytical overlay - AOL 140
anchoring 220
anger 45, 165
anxiety 45
attentional flexibility 34
auditory phenomena 88

B

Baars, Bernard 191
Bargh, John 96
baseline 67
beliefs 68, 159, 181
beta frequencies 32, 236
body 83
  ideomotor 107
body focus 38, 253, 263. *See* exercises
  spatial 65
brainwaves 32
bridging 39, 41

C

channels of awareness 37
clear intent 131
collective unconscious 81
color in healing 57
conscious awareness 81
consciousness 269
consciousness, layers 81
crystal balls 88

D

Dass, Ram 285
daydreaming 42
delta frequencies 32
De Quincey, Christian 71
description 253
description, value of 153
direct experience 126
direct perception 26–27, 57
doorways 23–27, 91
dowsing 108–119
drawing 173
dreams 42, 170

E

Edison, Thomas 95
emotional release 47
emotions
  anger 45, 165
  fear 181
emotions, charged 164, 182
entangled thinking 205
Erickson, Milton 64
Exceptional Human Experience 135

Exercises
  allowing intuition - target 135
  asking questions 229
  basic questions 116
  beginning sensing 29
  beliefs 68
  body focus as exploration 211
  body touch 248
  breathing 99
  breathing into the body 245
  conscious description 253
  deeper body focus 263
  describing 39
  direct perception 57
  drawing an object 78–80
  drawing senses 173
  enjoy an image 25
  enjoying the present moment 214
  envision an object 121
  envisioning the body 187
  expanding visualization 231
  experiences at the edge 49
  fascination 43
  feedback 102
  future sensing 157
  imagining and perceiving 53
  imagining space 32
  integrating the body 186
  intention and body 239
  intuitive perception 100
  intuitive process 141
  intuitive target 203
  money energy 227
  pendulum 110
  peripheral practice 258
  personal intuition questions 276
  personal suggestions 195
  personal validation 45
  playing with objects 224
  reaching out with intuition - telephone 149
  refining senses 250
  sense an object 74
  shifting focus 31
  softening the conscious mind 62
  sound perception 216
  spatial body focus 65
  spontaneous shifting states 41
  sticky fingers 118
  suggestion 191
  timed sensing 254
  tracing 76–78
  trance and sensing 85
  unconscious messaging 144–145
  visual focus 89
expectation 154
eye disorder 34

F

fascination 163
fear 181
feedback 102, 138–140
Fehmi, Les 32, 34
flow states 236–237
forensics 183, 184, 222–223

G

ghost hunting 184
God 71, 273
groups, working with 279

H

Harmin, Willis 202
Hatha Yoga 97
Huxley, Aldous 250
hypnagogic 183, 209, 219, 221
hypnotherapy 242
hypnotic susceptibility 32
hypnotic trance 34

I

ideomotor signals 107–119
imagination 53
immersed experience 126, 236–237
I'm OK 45
India 273
insomnia 34
intention 92, 124

body awareness 239
clear 131
strength 49
unconscious 165, 241
intention and perception 125
intuitive experiences 48, 50
intuitive process 141
Isenmen, Lois 96

J

Jaegers, Beverly 222–223
Jung, Carl 83

K

Kekule, August 95
kinesthetic 223
kinesthetic perceptions 89

L

landscape, using 269
layers of consciousness 81
levity 201
Lewis-Williams, David 88

M

Maharshi, Ramana 208, 273
mandala 89
mantra 273
marbles, holding 95
McMullen, George 222, 229
meditation 49
Mindell, Arnold 256–257
Mishlove, Jeffrey 110
money 227

N

Native American 97, 229
nature 269
needs 156
newspaper 173
noise 159

O

open focus 32, 34

P

peak experience 126, 177, 273–275
pendulum 108–119
perception 53, 125
  changes 23–24, 87
peripherals 258
portal. *See* doorways
psychometry 221, 224, 227

Q

questions, asking 267

R

radionics 110
remote viewing 144
resistance 46
Robbins, Jim 32
Rumi 73, 275

S

sacred 71
seeing 250
Selver, Charlotte 51, 70
sensory awareness 70
shamanism 205
skin disorder 34
sleep 45
sound 29
sound perception 216
sounds 88
space 219, 235
spirit 71
spiritual path 207
state markers 219
states of consciousness 219
stomach 108
stress 242, 247
suggestion 191

T

Tart, Charles 183–184
telepathy 49, 97
telephone 149
theta frequencies 32
timed sensing 254
touch 248
trance 64, 84
  phenomena 92

U

unconscious 43, 50, 81, 95, 241, 242
unconscious messaging 144–145

V

validation process. *See* personal
    validation
Vevekananda, Swami 273
vision 250
vision quest 97
vocabulary, building 254
voice, using the 231

W

Watson, Lyall 224
White, Rhea 135
writing 24, 39, 102

Y

yoga
  Hatha 97

Give the gift of *A Joyful Intuition*.
Check Your Local Bookstore or Order Here

◊ I want _____ copies of *A Joyful Intuition* for $17.99 each.

◊ I am interested in having Patrick Marsolek speak or give a seminar to my company, association, school or organization. Please send me information.

Include $4.00 shipping and handling for one book, and $2.00 for each additional book. Canadian orders must include payment in US funds, with 7% GST added.
Payment must accompany orders. Allow 3 weeks for delivery.

My check or money order for $_____ is enclosed.

Please charge my ◊ Visa ◊ Mastercard

Name_____
Address_____
City/State/Zip_____
Phone_____E-mail_____
Card #_____
Exp. Date_____Name on Card_____

Make your checks payable and return to:

Inner Workings Resources
P.O. Box 1264
Helena, MT 59624

**More Books & Audio CDs at:
www.InnerWorkingsResources.com**

www.ingramcontent.com/pod-product-compliance
Lightning Source LLC
Chambersburg PA
CBHW032039090426
42744CB00004B/66